Echoes
of Love

STORIES OF PREGNANCY
LOSS AND HEARTACHE

BECAUSE EVERY
HEARTBEAT, EVERY LOSS,
AND EVERY MEMORY
DESERVES TO BE
REMEMBERED

JAYME LEE BESS

Printed in the United States of America

Published in Hellertown, PA

Library of Congress Control Number available upon request

ISBN 979-8-89420-068-2

For more information or to place bulk orders, contact the author or the publisher at Jennifer@BrightCommunications.net.

Bright
COMMUNICATIONS

To the little soul who flickered in and out of my life before I ever had the chance to know you and to my precious twins, whose hearts once beat beneath mine: Your presence was brief, but your impact eternal.

Though you were with me only for a short while, you are etched into every corner of my heart. I carry you in the silence between breaths, in the ache that never fully leaves, and in the love that continues to grow even in your absence.

I am your mother. That truth cannot be erased by time, by distance, or by loss. You will always be with me, never forgotten.

This book is for you. It is my way of giving you a voice, of ensuring that your lives, no matter how short, were not silenced. Through these pages, I honor you and all the others whose mothers had to say goodbye before hello.

To anyone who has loved and lost, may you find the courage to speak your truth, to carry your love forward, and to believe that even through brokenness, your heart can find hope again.

Contents

Preface

Pregnancy loss is a grief so intimate, so silent, that many of us carry it in the quiet corners of our hearts, unseen, unspoken, but unbearably real.

If you are holding this book, chances are you know this kind of grief. Maybe you lost a baby you never got to hold, or maybe you said goodbye before you even got to say hello. Maybe you are sitting in the thick of it now, or maybe it's been years, and the ache still lingers like it was yesterday. No matter where you are in this journey, know this:

You are not alone.

This book was born from that shared ache—from the stories we don't always have the heart to tell. The kind that lives in ultrasound photos never framed, in due dates that pass quietly, in names we whisper only to ourselves.

The stories in this book are *real, raw, and honest.* They are the lived experiences of women who have walked through the devastation of loss and chosen to speak their truth, not to relive the pain, but to let you know you are not alone.

The truth is *so* many of us experience this. *Quietly. Privately.* The hardest part? The **what ifs**. What if I had done something differently? What if their heart kept beating? What if I never get to try this again?

The what ifs haunt us. They linger long after the appointments stop and the sympathy fades.

Grab some tissues because in these pages you will find echoes of your own heartbreak. You'll also find hope, not because we've moved on, but because we moved forward, carrying our babies and stories with us.

This book is a collection of voices, each one a light in the dark, reminding you that grief shared is grief softened. That healing isn't linear. That strength looks different on all of us. But most of all, that love, even in loss, is never wasted.

We are in this together.

May these stories hold space for your tears, your anger, your memories, your healing. May they remind you that your story matters and that sometimes life just isn't fair.

May you be gentle with yourself and always remember,

You are not alone.

All my love, Jayme

Introduction

Now, let's move onto the stories.

Each one comes from a place of truth. Some tender, some raw, all real. These are the voices of women who have experienced pregnancy loss and have chosen to share their journeys, not for sympathy, but to help others feel seen and to remind each of us that we are not alone in this pain.

The first story is mine. It's the story of two pregnancies, one brief and heartbreaking, the other full of hope and dreams that ended far too soon. Writing it was not easy, but sharing it feels like the most honest way to begin.

Get those tissues ready!! Here we go **together**, one story at a time.

Two Heartbeats, One Goodbye

I was 39 when I saw two pink lines on a test that I almost didn't take. I hadn't been trying. I hadn't been expecting. But there it was: life suddenly growing inside me. I blinked at the test, shocked at what I saw. Then I blinked again. I sat there in silence as all the emotions came running in.

Was this really happening? It had been almost 10 years since my daughter was born. I thought our family was complete. Then a smile spread across my face, and hope rushed in. We were all so excited to bring a new life into our home.

That pregnancy ended just four days later.

"Spontaneous abortion," the doctors said. Common. A fluke.

I tried to absorb the cold clinical words, but all I could feel was the strange emptiness of having something and then nothing. It felt like being handed a gift and having it taken away before I'd even untied the ribbon.

Still, I told myself to move on. I had barely been pregnant, right? But my heart didn't quite agree.

Then, almost miraculously, I was pregnant again. This time, it was different. It felt stronger. The lines were brighter. My numbers doubled, and everything looked great.

Then came the first ultrasound, **TWO** heartbeats!

TWINS!

I smiled as tears ran down my cheeks. My double rainbow! The universe, in some poetic twist, had made up for the pain of that first loss with a multiplied promise. Two little sparks growing inside me, fluttering heartbeats on a screen. It was everything I didn't know I needed.

The first trimester was a blur of cautious joy and quiet fear. I talked to them in whispers. I dreamed of who they would be; one fiery, one soft, or maybe both wild, bold, and feral like their momma. I imagined their nursery, their birthdays, their laughs, their milestones. I hadn't felt that whole in a long time. They were perfect, tiny, but real. *Moving. Growing. Alive.* I was overjoyed.

I spent endless hours over the next few weeks wondering how I'd tell the rest of our family. Halloween was approaching, my favorite holiday! I knew that was the perfect time to announce it. So I got on Amazon and purchased the cutest shirt that read, "Boo! We're Having Two!" So cute and oh so perfect. I couldn't wait to wear it.

October 26, 2023, at 12 weeks in, everything changed. I went in to my exam expecting to see them wiggling, stronger, bigger. But when the wand touched my belly and the screen lit up, I knew something was wrong.

The room fell silent. There was no movement, no sound. The ultrasound tech was quiet, too quiet. I looked up at her and asked her to be real with me, are my babies okay?

Her next words crushed me, "I'm sorry, but I can't detect any heartbeats." I had lost them both. She left the room. I sat there in stillness, the sterile gel cooling on my skin, my body still cradling them, unaware that their little hearts had stopped beating.

That moment is frozen in time. A surreal fracture in my life. Two lives lost, just like that.

The grief that followed was not linear. It came in waves; some gentle, some crashing. I went through the motions: appointments, decisions, the D&C (on Halloween of all days), and the healing. But nothing prepared me for the emotional void that followed.

I looked fine on the outside. I smiled, I worked, I showed up, but inside I was screaming. People didn't know what to say. Some said, "It just wasn't meant to be" and tried to comfort me with the "Everything happens for a reason." Others avoided the topic altogether. But I needed to talk. I needed them to count, not to be dismissed. They were real. They were mine, and then they were gone.

I only have one photo of them, the ultrasound image taken at eight weeks. Two small shadows. That image is all I have left to prove they were ever here, the only thing I will ever be able to hold. Sometimes I stare at it and wonder what could have been, what should have been. Who they would have become. What their laughs would have sounded like and what they would have fought over.

I carry them with me always. In quiet moments. In the ache behind my smile. In the way I touch my belly without thinking. In the dreams I still have where I'm holding them, where we're walking hand in hand, laughing. I think of them often, never allowing their memory to fade.

Pregnancy loss is an invisible grief. It's tucked away behind whispered condolences and silent tears. But I want to say their existence mattered. Their ending mattered.

If you've lost a pregnancy, no matter how early or how late, I want you to know: Your grief is valid. Your story matters. You are not alone.

I will forever be the mother of twins who never took a breath, but who took mine away the moment I heard their hearts beat. I will love and remember them for the rest of my life.

Remembering Baby Bumpy

Infertility is a quiet thief. It creeps into your life and rearranges everything you thought you knew about hope, timing, and control. It affects one in six people globally, but the statistics can never truly capture the way it carves its mark into your heart.

For me, infertility meant needles, schedules, IVF cycles, a miracle followed by disappointments, and the constant, fragile balance between daring to dream and bracing for heartbreak.

Still, despite the scars of the journey, there was always a tiny flame of hope. When we decided to try for a sibling for our IVF miracle boy, I let myself dream again. I pictured their little hands holding each other's. I imagined giggles echoing through our home, messy breakfasts, and the beautiful chaos of having two little ones. When our frozen embryo transfer was complete, I whispered to the tiny life inside me, "You are so wanted. You are so loved already." We nicknamed this baby "Baby Bumpy." It felt sweet and perfect, a name just for us, a promise of the bond we were building.

In the days leading up to our ultrasound, I prayed harder than I had in a long time. I envisioned the moment we'd see that tiny flicker on the screen, the heartbeat that would confirm my whispered promises were reaching them. I imagined the relief flooding through my body, replacing years of fear with joy. We allowed ourselves to think about baby names, nursery colors/themes, our future together. One of our favorite memories was how our older child reacted when we told him he was going to be a big brother.

The ultrasound room was quiet except for the hum of the machine. I lay there, holding my breath, searching the screen for the tiniest pulse of light. But the monitor stayed still. The silence in the room grew heavy, too heavy, until the doctor's voice confirmed what my heart had already begun to fear. There was no heartbeat.

In that instant, every dream I had dreamt unraveled. My body felt cold, my chest heavy. I wanted to run from the room, yet I couldn't move. I wanted to scream, yet no sound came out. I had prayed so hard, and still, my arms remained empty.

And then, the world around me seemed to collapse in more ways than one. The Covid-19 pandemic had brought the world to a standstill, hospitals filled with fear and rules, and loved ones kept at a distance. The very moment I needed someone to hold me, to help me stand when my knees buckled, I was told I had to face it alone. No visitors. No hand to squeeze. No shoulder to cry into.

The physical pain came later, sudden and merciless followed by a pool of blood. I had to be rushed to the hospital. There I hemorrhaged in silence, alone in a sterile white room, my life hanging in the balance. The walls closed in as my thoughts swirled: anger, confusion, disbelief, and a hollow ache that seemed to come from the deepest part of me. Time blurred. There was no day or night, only the relentless awareness that I was leaving the hospital without my baby.

In the weeks and months that followed, the world outside moved on, but mine remained cracked. Infertility and pregnancy loss don't just take your energy, your plans, or your money; they alter your heart. They change how you see families in the park, how you react to birth announcements, how you measure time. They weave grief into everyday moments, minimizing the joy we are supposed to feel for others.

Some days, I could smile at memories of the short time I had with Baby Bumpy: the way my heart leapt at the positive test, the soft hope I carried inside me. Other days, I couldn't breathe past the weight of what I'd lost. I learned that grief doesn't come in clean stages; it loops back on itself, catching you off guard when you least expect it.

Still, I hold onto the truth that Baby Bumpy existed. They were here, even for a brief moment, and they were loved fiercely. That love hasn't gone anywhere. It's etched into who I am now.

That's why this book matters so much. It gives those of us who have walked through this silent storm a space to speak our truth. To say to others: *You are not alone.* To honor the babies we carry in our hearts instead of our arms. And to stand together in both grief and hope.

Baby Bumpy may never have taken a breath in this world, but they left an imprint I will carry forever. My love for them is stitched into every prayer, every tear, and every whispered, "I miss you."

Always remembered. Always loved.

For Baby Bumpy.

Lily and Lucy

The ultrasound room smelled faintly of hand sanitizer and something sterile, like new plastic. The lights were dim, and the hum of the machine filled the air as the sonographer moved the probe across my belly.

"Oh," she said softly, eyes darting to the screen. "You're having two."

My heart jumped into my throat.

When the sonographer turned the monitor toward me, I saw them: two tiny flickers of light pulsing in perfect rhythm. My eyes blurred with tears. My husband reached for my hand, squeezing until my knuckles whitened, and I could feel his breath catch in his chest.

We laughed and cried at the same time. Twins. A double miracle.

We named them that night, Lily and Lucy. We said their names out loud in the dark, letting the syllables roll off our tongues until they felt like part of us. I pictured them in matching pajamas, their little feet pattering down the hallway in the mornings. I imagined chaos and giggles and a love so big our house could barely hold it.

But joy is fragile.

At my next appointment, the doctor's face changed before he even spoke. He was trying to be gentle, but I saw the truth in his eyes. Lucy's heart had stopped.

My world tilted. I clutched the table as if I could keep everything from slipping away.

The doctor explained that we should leave her where she was to give Lily the best chance. My heart shattered, but I agreed. I told myself I could carry them both, even if one was only with me in silence. I would keep them together as long as I could.

Carrying life and death inside you is an impossible weight. Every kick from Lily felt like a small victory, but every stretch of quiet reminded me of Lucy's absence. Some nights, I rested my hand on my belly and whispered to both of them. I wanted Lucy to know she was still loved.

Then came the fever.

It started as an ache in my back, then chills, then a heat that seemed to crawl under my skin and burn me from the inside out. At my exam, the nurse took one look at me and called the doctor. I was given an IV before I could even form the question: What's wrong?

It was an infection. Bacteria from losing Lucy had spread, and it was attacking my body. The word *sepsis* was mentioned. The phrase *life-threatening* followed soon after.

The doctor sat on the edge of the bed, voice low. "We need to end the pregnancy. If we don't … you may not survive."

I stared at him, the words hitting me like stones. End the pregnancy. End Lily's life to save my own. I wanted to say no. I wanted to bargain, to scream, to beg. But my husband was gripping my hand so tightly I could feel his silent plea, *Stay alive.*

And so I signed the papers.

The rest of that day is a blur of fluorescent lights, the beeping of machines, and the faint sound of a nurse humming to herself as she adjusted my blanket. At one point, I turned my head toward the window and saw rain streaking the glass. It felt right somehow, like the sky knew how to grieve with me.

When it was over, the silence inside my body was deafening.

I came home with empty arms. The nursery we'd only just started was left half-finished, a crib leaning against the wall, unopened boxes stacked in the corner. I couldn't go inside.

Life around me didn't stop. The traffic still roared past the house. Neighbors still mowed their lawns. Even the seasons had the audacity to change, the air turning crisp as fall crept in. But I was frozen in place.

My husband and I began to fray. Grief is cruel like that. It worms its way into the small spaces between you, twisting your words, turning love into hate. We snapped at each other over dishes, over laundry, over nothing at all. But really, we were snapping at the emptiness.

Friends and family said, "We're so sorry. We're here for you." I know they meant it, but the words bounced off me. Nothing they could say would change the fact that my babies were gone. Sometimes silence was easier than awkward kindness.

At night, I dreamed of them. I saw Lily with her father's dark hair, Lucy with my eyes. I imagined them learning to walk, chasing each other in the yard, fighting over toys, blowing out birthday candles. I woke up with the ghost of those moments clinging to me like mist.

I'm not ready to move on. I don't even know what that means anymore.

I read somewhere that grief is love with nowhere to go. If that's true, then maybe this ache is just my love for them, too big to disappear, too heavy to carry without stumbling.

I carried my children. I loved them before I ever saw their faces. And even though they never took a breath, they will always be mine.

Always.

My Angel, My Saving Grace

I never imagined that joy could arrive so quietly. No fanfare, no rush of people clapping me on the back, just a blood test and a nurse's gentle words, "You're pregnant."

It was 2009, and by then, I had long stopped expecting miracles. Seven years earlier, in the spring of 2002, I had been certain motherhood would come easily. I was young, and although my body had its share of problems—heavy cycles, discomfort that flared and ebbed—I thought time was my ally. One year later, that illusion dissolved. Tests revealed the truth: cysts, endometriosis, precancerous cells. My reproductive system was already a battlefield.

I believed surgery would be my way out, that each procedure was a step toward cradling my child. But the years that followed told another story. Between 2003 and 2008, miscarriages became an unwanted rhythm in my life. Some happened so early that I'd barely had time to whisper *I'm pregnant* before it was over.

The hospital bed I occupied in 2009 wasn't for a pregnancy. It was for something else entirely. I wasn't thinking about babies when they drew my blood that morning. But when the nurse returned, smiling gently, my world shifted.

Barely pregnant, they told me. I didn't care. My heart knew no "barely." Life was life.

I had been with the man I loved for a year by then, a man who had stepped into my life after I had clawed my way out of a violent marriage. He was tender, patient, everything my past had not been. We rejoiced in whispers, holding our happiness between us like something fragile. We prayed. We dreamed. For seven days, the hospital was our nursery of hope.

On the eighth morning, I woke to pain. Not the dull ache I was used to, but something deeper, sharper. My hand found the sheets and came away wet. Red spread across the bed, blooming fast. My boyfriend had already gone to work. I pressed the nurse's call button with shaking fingers.

The nurse came quickly and helped me sit up, her face calm but her movements quick. A doctor ordered an ultrasound. The hallway to the imaging room felt colder than it should have. In the dim light of the exam room, the tech moved the wand across my belly. I searched her face for answers, but she gave none. The monitor showed only stillness.

The doctor entered. His voice was a scalpel: precise, cutting, and cold. "Your baby has no heartbeat." No pause. No softening. No apology. He turned and walked out as if my grief were an inconvenience to his day.

A week earlier, my boyfriend and I had been planning a future with our child. Now I sat in a sterile room with the soundless absence of a heartbeat echoing in my chest. I had to tell him our baby was gone. It would have been his first child. It would have been our first together.

The grief hollowed us both. Our family tried to comfort us but failed. "At least you weren't far along," they said, as if the number of days could measure the size of love. We had no one to hold us up, and eventually, the weight of our loss broke what we had built. We lost our baby, and we lost each other.

The years that followed were quiet in all the wrong ways. Loss became something I wore in my bones. Infertility, early menopause. Those words defined my body. I had always dreamed of a house full of children. In 2018 when I researched IVF, I learned that as a single woman with diminished ovarian reserve, I would need both an egg and sperm donor to create embryo. The cost was an iron gate I couldn't climb.

So I prayed. I asked God to guide me, to show me if motherhood would ever be part of my path. And then, in 2022, I read about embryo adoption, couples donating unused embryos so others might have the children they longed for. I joined an online group in 2024, hesitant but curious. That's where I first heard about Acts of Kindness (AOK) Embryo Donation.

In February 2025, I filled out an inquiry. I was cautious, unsure if I could afford it, unsure if I would even be considered. But then I met Jayme and Shalistar. From the first conversation, they felt like family—two women who had also walked through grief and came out still holding compassion in their hearts.

That month, I adopted my first embryo. The road to transfer was rocky with health scares, delays, and moments when I doubted I'd even make it to the procedure. But Jayme and Shalistar were there every step, their faith steady when mine wavered.

By June 30, I was cleared. On July 12, I underwent my first frozen embryo transfer. I was hopeful. I was ready.

But a few days later, unease crept in. Something felt wrong. On July 22, the phone call confirmed it: my beta was negative. My embryo had not implanted. I told myself I had prepared for this, but grief still came, quiet and relentless. On July 30, the cramps began, followed by bleeding. This time, I kept my sorrow hidden behind smiles, but inside, I was unraveling. I blamed myself. Had I lifted too much? Stressed too much?

Jayme refused to let me drown in guilt. She prayed with me. She understood. She reminded me that this little embryo, though here for only a moment, had still touched my life.

And she was right. That tiny spark of life had given me something unexpected: a family within the AOK community, a sister in Jayme, and the courage to try again. God had guided me to this place, and now, I am preparing for another transfer in the fall of 2025.

I have learned that no matter how far along, a loss is still a loss. Every soul matters. My angels were too precious for this world, but they were my saving grace. I will carry them always! Their love, their footprints, etched forever in my heart.

The Day the Floor Turned Brown

My daughter was two and a half years old when the two pink lines appeared. It was early, just a week past my missed period, but I already felt the warm rush of possibility move through me. We had been trying, hoping, praying, and here it was, tangible proof that life was beginning inside me.

We told everyone almost right away, somewhere around five or six weeks in. Our joy felt too big to keep inside. But when we shared the news, the reactions didn't match the way my heart was soaring. Family offered careful smiles or shifted uncomfortably in their seats. Mixed emotions, you'd say.

It hurt, more than I cared to admit at the time, but we carried our excitement anyway. We told our daughter too. At her age, she didn't quite understand the meaning of *sibling*, but she smiled and wrapped her little arms around me. That was enough.

The weeks moved gently forward until the morning I was mopping the bathroom floor. It was hot with sunlight pouring through the window in bright sheets of gold. I wore a loose sundress, the kind that swishes lightly against the skin, as I moved across the white tile in an easy rhythm.

Scrub. Scrub. Scrub.

The bristles of the mop scraped faintly, a sound so ordinary it barely registered, until I noticed something else. Small brown dots speckled the tile I'd just cleaned. At first,

I thought it might be dirt I'd missed, but when I bent closer, my chest tightened.

No.

I straightened up quickly, the mop handle still in my hand, willing the moment to pass like a shadow moving over a wall. But then came more. Not just a few spots, now a trail. A spreading truth I didn't want to accept.

In an instant, the faint tug of nausea that had been my companion for days disappeared. The heaviness in my breasts, the subtle warmth low in my belly—all of it seemed to drain out of me as if someone had pulled a plug.

Three hours later, I was bleeding heavily.

The ER was cold in a way that had nothing to do with the temperature. The fluorescent lights hummed overhead, flattening everything into pale shades of blue and gray. I lay on the narrow bed, the paper-thin sheet crinkling under me, my hands clenched tight against my stomach.

They drew my blood. The nurse's voice was brisk, efficient, as she read the results. My HCG levels had dropped. I was actively miscarrying.

That was it. No pause for kindness, no hand on my shoulder, no space for the weight of the moment. Just the quick shuffle of feet out the door as they moved on to the next patient.

I was a number. A chart to be signed. A bed to be cleared.

When the nurse handed me my discharge papers, it was without instruction on how to take care of myself. No resources for grief, no words for the emptiness I was walking out with. The sliding glass doors opened to the night air, and I stepped into a world that kept moving as if nothing had changed. But everything had.

That baby mattered to me. Still does. I carry them in the quiet corners of my heart, a name I never got to speak aloud, a face I never got to see.

At home, I told myself I needed to keep going. My daughter still needed me whole. I had to learn how to live with the loss without letting it hollow me completely. Some days, that meant pretending I was fine until I almost believed it. Other days, it meant sitting alone in the bathroom, letting the ache roll through me in waves.

I tried to tell myself what I've always believed: What's meant to be will happen. Maybe there was a reason, though I couldn't see it from where I stood in the wreckage. It wasn't an answer, but it was something to hold onto when the silence felt too big.

The truth is, losing a baby is never something you "get over." The pain settles into you, changes you, becomes part of the way you see the world. But you can learn to carry it. And you can lean on others who have walked this road, even if the only thing they can offer is the knowing look that says, *I see you. I've been there.*

To those who have felt this kind of heartbreak, big hugs and all my love. You are not alone.

Two Hearts, Two Days, One Bond

In the weeks before Hannah was born, life felt like a gentle waiting.

I remember the quiet rituals of those days: the way I'd rest my hands over my belly and feel her soft, rolling movements beneath my palms, like a secret only we shared. Mornings came slow, the sunlight stretching through the curtains and warming the quilt at my feet. I'd hum to her sometimes, a tune without words, not knowing if she could hear it but hoping she felt it.

There was so much imagining in those days. I pictured the shape of her mouth, whether she would have my eyes or her father's. I dreamed of holding her against my chest, of breathing in that newborn scent everyone talks about, of learning the tiny sounds that would mean I'm hungry or I'm tired or I'm safe here.

I didn't know, couldn't have known, how quickly that gentle waiting could shatter. How one moment could split your life into before and after so suddenly that you barely have time to understand what's happening.

The day Hannah came into the world, the air in the delivery room felt heavier than I'd ever known it could be. It was as if time had slowed to a crawl, each second stretching long and thin, as fragile as the breath I prayed she would take.

She was early, just 32 weeks. That wasn't our birth plan. Nothing about that day followed the plan.

The morning had begun quietly, almost deceptively so. I remember the muted hum of the hospital corridors, the faint antiseptic tang in the air, the beeping of machines that would soon become the rhythm of our days. Then the rupture; a placental abruption, the doctors said later, tore through the quiet like a crack of thunder.

They think it was the sudden onset of preeclampsia. I only knew that something had shifted inside me, knowing deep in my bones that life as I understood it was slipping away.

When she was born, my sweet girl had already been without air for who knows how long. Each second now felt like an eternity. The room was filled with the hushed urgency of nurses and doctors, voices low but firm, moving with the precision of people fighting for a life. I clung to hope like a lifeline, my mind repeating her name silently, over and over.

And then, she fought! My God, she fought.

Our Hannah, impossibly small yet fierce, stayed with us. They placed her in the NICU, the room aglow with the soft blue of monitors, wires tracing delicate paths across her tiny body. Her breaths were shallow but present, her heartbeat a whisper of defiance.

Those two days in the NICU were the longest and shortest days of my life. Every morning, I'd press my hands to the clear walls of her isolette before slipping them inside to touch her. Her skin was soft, almost translucent, and warm under my fingertips. The hum and beep of the machines became a kind of lullaby, each sound a reminder that she was still here.

I told her everything. How much I loved her. How proud I was of her. How I wished I could have kept her safe inside me just a little longer.

And then, the day came. The day I still can't say without my chest tightening, my breath catching halfway. We had to say goodbye. Her tiny chest rose and fell for the last time in my arms, and the world felt like it tilted off its axis.

She was my first child. My first experience of motherhood. And yet, some mornings I wake up in disbelief, the weight of it pressing down as I realize, this is my life now. A life where my daughter exists in memory, in photographs, in the faint scent of her skin that I sometimes still imagine.

I read other stories now, from women and families who've walked this same unthinkable path. And though it doesn't erase the pain, there is comfort in knowing I am not alone in this strange, hollow grief. This is a community no one wants to join, yet here we are, bound by the love we have for the children we couldn't keep.

To those who share their hearts: thank you. I wish each of us peace. Not the kind that erases the ache, but the kind that makes it bearable, moment to moment, breath to breath.

The Day My World Tilted

Some stories don't start on the day everything changes. They start earlier, quietly, before you know you're in them.

It was mid-February when my dad called out of the blue, his voice holding that strange mix of hesitance and certainty that only comes when you're trying to explain something you can't quite name. "Would you feel comfortable taking a pregnancy test?" he asked. There was no small talk to soften it, no buildup. Just the question.

I laughed a little, caught between surprise and confusion. "I can. But I'd have to go buy one."

"Okay," he said, as if that settled something. "Later then."

That night, after work, I stopped at the store, slipping the test into my cart between shampoo and paper towels like it was nothing. At home, I took it, watched the window slowly fill, and saw only one line. Negative. I called my dad to tell him. No answer. I decided not to leave a photo on his phone for him to interpret in the dim hours of night. Some things were better said aloud.

Weeks passed without my father mentioning it again. Then, on March 9th, I visited for his birthday. Midway through the day, he caught me in the hallway. "What ever happened with that test?" he asked, never explaining why he wanted to know so badly.

"It was negative," I told him. He nodded, and we went back to celebrating.

But that night, the question lingered in my mind like a half-forgotten song. I dug through the bathroom drawer, found a test, and took it, half out of boredom, half out of a sense I couldn't name. Two bright, unshakable lines appeared.

I blinked and took another. Same thing. Two lines, defiant and sure.

My first call was to my best friend. "Tell me I'm not crazy," I said. She didn't. She confirmed what I already knew but couldn't quite believe.

The next morning at work, I couldn't keep it to myself. My sister-in-law, who also happened to be my boss, was the first I told. We stood in the break room, both of us teary-eyed, and she suggested I take a digital test. The minutes in that bathroom stretched into an eternity, the ticking of the clock louder than my own heartbeat. When the word *pregnant* appeared, followed by *3+ weeks*, my world tilted.

That evening, I packed a small box: tiny socks, a baby rattle, the tests. A quiet, tangible secret. My fiancé's eyes widened when he opened the gift, and we sat together in awe. For years, doctors had told me Polycystic Ovary Syndrome made this almost impossible. Yet here we were.

We began telling our family, each announcement making it more real. The joy was contagious.

March 19th: The first appointment, confirmation that this was truly happening.

April 3rd: The first time we saw our baby, no larger than a bean but infinitely more precious, life, new and unformed, flickering inside me.

April 23rd: Ten weeks. I lay on the exam table, cold paper crinkling beneath me, waiting for the doctor. He entered, and with a few words, "There's no heartbeat," my world shattered. No bleeding, no pain, no warning. Just silence.

I refused to accept it. We drove to the hospital for a second opinion. When the ultrasound tech turned the screen away, I knew. My body felt hollow, as if the air had been pulled from me. Then came the words *partial molar pregnancy*. Then the unthinkable, "This can sometimes become a rare cancer."

April 28th: The hospital called to schedule my D&C. The night was chaos. Needles, IVs, my veins resisting everything they tried.

April 29th: Surgery day. They said it would take 30 minutes. It took nearly two hours. I woke to news of heavy blood loss, more than in childbirth, and a long recovery ahead. My numbers kept dropping. My blood pressure sank. I drifted in and out, the edges of the world blurring. When I collapsed in a nurse's arms, they decided on a transfusion. My body rejected it. A second one was needed before my numbers finally rose.

Home was no easier. The nursery stood empty. For nearly two weeks, I could barely walk. Friends and family brought gifts, soft blankets, small tokens, but the one that stayed with me was a Build-A-Bear with my baby's heartbeat inside. I would press it to my ear when the nights became unbearable.

For months, I had to return for bloodwork and repeat the same explanation to nurses, "I need my HCG checked due to a miscarriage." Each time, it reopened something inside me.

My body has changed. I have changed. There's a line between who I was before and who I am now. The loss made me slower to rush through life, more intent on holding joy when it appears.

As my due date approaches, I think of my baby: Wrenlee Naomi if a girl. Lane Hunter if a boy. In their honor I am planning to get a tattoo, something permanent, so they'll always be with me.

And I want to say this to anyone who's been here: It is not the end. You are still a mother. Even if they're not in your arms, they're in your heart. And that makes you the strongest person you never knew you could be.

Empty in Every Way

The summer of 2014 was warm in a way that made the air feel almost golden. I can still remember the moment I learned Sofia was on her way, that sharp edge of surprise followed instantly by joy. We were going to have another girl. After six boys, she would be the third daughter in a row. *Blessings on blessings,* I thought. A trio of girls, hand in hand, growing up surrounded by their brothers' laughter and mischief.

The months passed easily at first. Every appointment with Sofia brought reassurance: She was growing, her heart was strong, and everything seemed fine. Later in the pregnancy, though, there were moments when her heart rate dipped, quick drops that made mine do the same. The doctors ran stress tests, monitoring her closely, and each time, her heartbeat rallied.

She's a fighter, I told myself. Every ultrasound showed a healthy little girl, and I let hope carry me forward.

The day before I was scheduled to be induced, I went to the hospital for monitoring. Sofia's heart still dipped now and then, but the nurses said it was nothing to worry about. The next morning, we arrived at the hospital ready to meet her... only to be told they were too busy.

"Come back tomorrow," they said.

So we went home, washed the baby clothes, double-checked the diaper bag, and tried to keep our excitement steady for one more day.

We left early the next morning. The hospital was cool and bright, smelling faintly of bleach and coffee. I changed into a gown, climbed onto the bed, and let the nurse attach the monitors. She pressed the Doppler to my belly, waiting for the galloping rhythm I'd come to love. Instead, there was silence. She frowned, pressed harder, shifted the wand. Nothing.

Another nurse came in, her voice hushed but urgent. Still nothing.

They wheeled in an ultrasound machine. The wand slid over my belly. The black-and-white images flickered on the screen, but no pulsing blur, no steady thump. The nurse's eyes softened in a way that told me before her words did.

"I'm so sorry," she said quietly. "She had a heartbeat yesterday ... but she doesn't anymore."

The nurse who had been there first began to cry. I could see she was trying to hold it in, but her tears came anyway. She told me I could have an epidural and deliver Sofia. My husband's hands trembled as he called our children and family.

They moved me to another floor. The air in that room was still in a way that felt unnatural, heavy. Family came in quietly, their voices barely above whispers. Eyes swollen, cheeks wet, we sat together in disbelief. I kept thinking about the life that had just vanished. All the hopes, the plans, the way I had pictured her fitting into our family, gone.

I was angry. I wanted them to do a C-section, to try something, *anything,* to save her. But it was already too late. Labor came in waves, but without the comfort of anticipating a cry at the end of it. When the family stepped out, it was just me, my husband, and Sofia.

She was silent when she arrived. I held her close, kissed her soft skin, rocked her like I could somehow coax her back. I sang to her "One Sweet Day," the words trembling out of me.

Even now, that song breaks me.

They dressed her in the tiny outfit I had brought for her first day. She was beautiful. "Now I Lay Me Down To Sleep" came and took photographs, gifting us a box of keepsakes. Her little hat held her scent for months afterward.

Leaving Sofia behind was like tearing myself in two. I didn't hold her one last time; my heart just couldn't bear it. The funeral was small, her body in a carrier. She wasn't tiny, nearly eight pounds, which somehow made it harder. I kept circling back to that one thought: *If they had taken her a day earlier, she would be here now.*

In the moments after, I learned that grief doesn't leave. It changes shape, settles into the corners of your life, and becomes a part of who you are. There's a before and an after, and you carry them both forever.

I honor Sofia each birthday and every October, lighting candles and sometimes playing "One Sweet Day" for her to hear, a gentle reminder that she was loved and will always be with us.

Olivia was my second heartbreak. Losing her felt different, lonelier somehow. She was known more by me than anyone else because we only had a short time with her.

It was supposed to be a routine visit.

I'd done this so many times before, lie back, gel on the belly, wait for the quick rhythm of her heartbeat to fill the room.

But the nurse was quiet.

Too quiet.

Her wand glided back and forth, back and forth, the cool gel spreading in thin streaks across my skin. She pressed harder, her eyes narrowing at the screen. My own eyes followed hers, searching for the familiar flicker.

There was none.

"She's measuring smaller than she should," she said softly, and her voice carried something heavy I didn't want to hear. She slipped out of the room to get the doctor.

The door opened again, and in walked truth wearing a stethoscope.

He didn't hesitate. Didn't wrap it in softness. "She passed about a week ago." The words landed like stones in my chest. He rushed back out of the room, indifferently, as if he hadn't just shattered my dreams.

I was alone when the air thickened, when the walls seemed to close in. Alone when my body folded in on itself, tears hot and unrelenting. My fingers fumbled at my clothes. My legs gave way in the hallway, and I gripped the wall just to keep from sinking to the floor.

They scheduled the D&C, told me I'd have time to process. But grief doesn't care about schedules.

Before the day came, I began to bleed.

In the still, suffocating quiet of our bathroom, pain seized me in waves. And then ... *It* happened.

Olivia slipped from me into the toilet.

I froze. My breath caught somewhere between my lungs and my throat. The room blurred at the edges.

My husband and oldest son, faces pale with grief, gently retrieved her and placed her into a small box so she wouldn't be taken from me completely. I held that box like it was the only thing tethering me to her.

But my body wasn't finished breaking. The bleeding didn't stop. Contractions came, sharp and merciless. My skin went cold, my vision tunneled.

At the hospital, hands worked quickly, voices sharpened with urgency. They tried to remove what was left, but my vitals crashed. The D&C became immediate, a race against my own body.

When I woke, there was a hollow ache where she had been—not just in my womb, but everywhere: my chest, my hands, my voice. I was emptied in a way no one warns you about.

Olivia's life was a whisper. She came and went before the world could know her name. And because the world didn't know her, it didn't grieve her, not the way they had grieved Sofia.

But she was mine. Entirely mine. And the weight of loving someone the world refuses to see is a loneliness I still carry.

Both my daughters took pieces of me with them. There's no returning to who I was before.

For anyone who faces this kind of loss, my only advice is this: Let yourself grieve. No one can tell you how or when. This was your baby. The world may move on, but you carry them forever. And though the ache never leaves, there will be moments when the sun feels warm again.

The Silence After Impact

I don't usually talk about myself. I don't open the door wide enough for anyone to see the mess inside. But this is different. This is my story, and my body still remembers it as if it happened yesterday.

Earlier this year, I found out I was pregnant with my first baby. My little boy. Each doctor's visit felt like a secret celebration, his tiny heart flickering on the monitor like a fragile candle in the dark, growing stronger, steady, unwavering. Every flutter inside me was a whisper of life, a reminder that something miraculous had taken root. I imagined December, a few days before Christmas, wrapped in warmth and twinkling lights, cradling him close. I would hum softly as he slept, tracing his tiny hands with my fingers, dreaming of the life we would share.

Summer arrived, unremarkable and ordinary, the kind of days that feel safe because nothing has yet betrayed you. The sky was a careful blue and the sunlight glinted across the streets as I drove, unaware of the fracture that would soon tear my world apart.

Then it came: the scream of tires on asphalt, the bone-deep grind of colliding metal, and the savage jolt that slammed me against the shards of steel and glass. Pain followed in waves. My hips felt splintered, my side throbbed in protest, my neck cried out with every movement, and my mind sank into a dizzying fog.

But through the chaos, one thought remained prominent: *My baby. Is he alive? Did I protect him enough from the impact of the crash?*

At the hospital, I was a collection of broken parts, fractures, injuries, bruises, but the worst was the anxiety that gripped my chest tighter than any seatbelt ever could. And yet, when the monitor first whispered his heartbeat, relief rushed through me like warm water over chilled skin. He was there. He survived when I felt utterly destroyed.

For the next 24 hours, I clung to that rhythm. Each beep, each flicker of light, tethered me to life. I traced my swollen belly with trembling fingers, whispering promises and prayers to a tiny boy I could not yet hold. The antiseptic smell of the hospital, the steady beeping of machines, the soft murmur of nurses' voices became background music to the miracle inside me. In those moments, hope felt almost tangible, as if I could cup it in my hands and shield it from the world.

Then came the next morning. The staff entered as always, calm and routine, but this time something shifted in the air, like the sudden drop in temperature before a storm. The probe pressed to my stomach. The monitor flickered. Silence.

"No heartbeat."

The words pierced me, hollowing me from the inside. Numbness spread, icy and unyielding. My body betrayed me in ways I could never have imagined. And then the miscarrying began. Pain unlike any I had ever known surged through me, sharp, deep, relentless waves that left me gasping, clutching at sheets soaked with more than just sweat. The accident had shattered my bones, but this, this stole my soul. My womb emptied. My sweet baby boy slipped away.

I felt hollow, a vessel of guilt and grief. My body, which I had hoped would be his protector, had failed him. Every throb of pain was a cruel reminder. Every time I closed my eyes, I saw the space where he should have been. I felt the absence where his life had been. I would never wish this emptiness, this guilt, on anyone.

The doctors say we can try again next month. And we will. We want to. Yet the thought twists my insides into knots. Moving forward is terrifying. To hope again feels like treachery. *Can I dream of another heartbeat without betraying the one I lost? Can joy coexist with grief, or will it always be tinged with shadows of guilt?*

I replay the crash endlessly in my mind: the smell of burnt rubber, the sharp tang of metal, the sudden jerk of my body, the metallic taste in my mouth, the blur of sirens, and the harsh fluorescence of the hospital lights above me. And I feel my boy's tiny heartbeat beneath my fingers—an echo now only in memory, tender and unreachable.

Yet, sometimes, in the quiet, I feel his presence. A whisper of the life that was, a reminder of the love that was never denied. I can close my eyes and still imagine his tiny fingers curling around mine, soft and perfect, as though he is still just beyond the veil of what is seen.

My grief is private, my guilt is intimate, but they are real. My story is one of pain, yes, but it's also one of fragile hope, of the aching resilience that refuses to let go completely, even when everything feels broken. And so I breathe, one trembling breath at a time, holding the space for both sorrow and the possibility of joy, hoping that one day they can coexist.

I will never be the same, but even in my brokenness, I am still here, still breathing, still reaching for the light and hoping for a brighter tomorrow.

The Test I'll Never Forget

I found out I was pregnant in May of 2022. It had been eight years since my daughter was born, and only after she grew older did I finally decide I was ready to try again.

For months, the tests were negative. Each morning and sometimes even throughout the day, I would test too early, hoping the lines would change. It became a routine of longing, of squinting at plastic sticks under bathroom lights, praying for something different.

I was working at Walmart then, and one afternoon on my lunch break I picked up another test. I carried it to the bathroom, took it quickly, and stuffed it back into my bag. I couldn't bear to look at it right there, under harsh fluorescent lights. When my shift ended, I walked to my car, closed the door, and finally let myself look. The word *pregnant* stared back at me. Two lines, bold and undeniable. My hands shook, but my heart soared.

After eight years, after months of disappointment, it was finally happening again. I was overjoyed. Unlike my first pregnancy, there was no fear. No worry. I embraced it fully, smiling to myself as I imagined my daughter's face when I told her she was finally going to be a big sister. For once, I felt free of the anxious shadow that had followed me before.

The only frustration was waiting. The women's center wouldn't schedule my first appointment until I was further along, and the weeks dragged by like years. Desperate for reassurance, I searched and found a clinic that would do an early ultrasound. I was just five weeks, and the image they gave me didn't show much, but it showed enough. A tiny speck. A promise. Those blurry black-and-white photos were all I had, the first and only pictures of that baby.

By seven weeks, the first sign of trouble appeared. It was just a small streak of blood at first, but enough to make my heart stop. My doctor sent me for bloodwork, checking my HCG levels over several days. The numbers weren't climbing the way they should. I tried to hold on to hope, scouring the internet for stories of women who bled early and still carried healthy pregnancies. But deep down, I think I already knew.

At work, I kept running to the bathroom to check, each time praying the bleeding had stopped. But by noon that day, at eight weeks, my fears came true. In a cold, sterile stall of a Walmart bathroom, I miscarried. I passed what was left of the baby I had longed for, a baby that had stopped growing at just six and a half weeks.

I felt numb. My body was in shock, but I wasn't allowed to leave work. The rest of the day blurred together, like I was moving through water, detached and hollow. What consumed me most was not even myself, but the thought of telling my daughter, knowing how badly she wanted a sibling and how much she would hurt too.

I longed to go home, to grieve in private, to curl myself around my daughter and let her presence anchor me. Instead, I felt trapped in a place where grief wasn't allowed to take up space, where I had to keep moving when my whole world had stopped.

In the days and weeks after, shame began to creep in. I wondered if I had done something wrong, if I had caused this. I replayed everything in my mind: what I ate, what I lifted, what I worried about. My body had let go of my baby, and I couldn't shake the blame. All I had left were a few ultrasound photos and the pregnancy test I had saved. Nothing more, because it ended too soon.

That loss changed me. It unlocked a level of anxiety I never knew existed. A month later, I found myself staring at another positive test, this time with the baby who would become my son. But joy never came the way I expected it to. Instead, fear shadowed every step. Each time I went to the bathroom, I paused, bracing myself for blood. Every day hope battled terror. I carried him, but I also carried the memory of what I had lost and the fear that it could happen again.

Somehow, I made it through. My daughter's kind and gentle heart gave me strength in the darkest days. She needed me, and caring for her gave me purpose. And that second positive test, fragile as it felt, gave me something to look toward when grief threatened to swallow me.

The loss of that baby will always stay with me. The tiny heartbeat that never had the chance to grow left an imprint on my soul. I carry both, the ache of loss and the fierce love for the children I hold in my arms. One doesn't erase the other. They exist together, forever, in the silence between heartbeats.

From Tears to Blessings

The second time around, Jeremy and I thought we had it all perfectly planned. Kameron, our firstborn, was just two years old, and we dreamed of a sibling close in age. We timed everything carefully, and when the pregnancy test turned positive, it felt like the world had aligned with our hopes. The baby was due in early September, exactly as we had imagined.

We were overjoyed. We began buying little clothes and soft blankets, filling drawers with tiny things that made the dream feel so real. One of the first things I picked out was a "Baby's First Christmas" sleeper. I remember holding it up in the store, picturing a chubby-cheeked baby wearing it as lights twinkled on the tree. That sleeper still sits folded away, unworn, a tender reminder of the dreams we had and the loss we would later endure.

This pregnancy felt different from my first. With Kameron, morning sickness had been relentless, day and night, leaving me weak and frail. I lost 12 pounds before I ever began to gain any weight. But this time, my body felt calm, steady, and strong. It almost seemed too good to be true. Then the spotting began. Just light streaks of blood, but enough to knot my stomach with worry.

I visited the obstetrician again and again, explaining what I saw, my fears tumbling out faster each time. But each visit brought a different provider, and their answers never changed: Spotting can be normal during pregnancy. Still, my heart whispered something else, a quiet alarm I couldn't silence.

Finally, one doctor suggested an ultrasound. As the screen lit up, there it was, our baby. I saw the flicker of a heartbeat, steady and strong, and tears filled my eyes. The sound of that rhythm, so fragile yet so sure, wrapped itself around my soul. In that moment, I fell even deeper in love. I left the office with renewed hope, carrying that heartbeat with me like a promise. The doctor placed me on bedrest, and I obeyed, spending that evening stretched out on the couch, cradled by cautious optimism.

That night, cramps gnawed at my stomach, sharper than before, but I reminded myself of the heartbeat. I clung to it like an anchor. *Everything will be fine,* I told myself.

The next morning, Jeremy had already left for work, and Kameron, now three years old, came bouncing into my room, asking for something to drink. My mom was already on her way, making the 35-minute drive to help care for Kameron so I could rest. I hadn't even gotten out of bed yet, but the cramps were worse. When I finally stood, intending only to get my daughter her drink, I felt a sudden rush of fluid.

My heart plummeted. I knew in an instant what was happening.

I staggered to the bathroom, hands trembling, tears pouring before the words could even form. I called my mom, sobbing so hard I could barely breathe, and begged her to hurry. Then, with shaking hands, I called Jeremy. My voice cracked as I told him what was happening, the finality of it cutting through every syllable.

As I sat waiting for my mom to arrive, thoughts crashed through my mind like waves in a storm: *What did I do wrong? I shouldn't have stood up. I shouldn't have gotten out of bed. My baby is gone. My life is over. How can I keep on living?*

And then just as the weight of despair threatened to crush me, my three-year-old daughter climbed into my lap. She wrapped her tiny arms around me, hugged me with all her strength, and whispered, "I love you."

It was as if God Himself spoke through her in that moment—a reminder that though I had lost one child, I still had another who needed me. Another who loved me fiercely, who gave me a reason to keep breathing through the pain.

At the hospital, Jeremy met me, his face etched with grief and helplessness. My mom sat in the waiting room with Kameron, while I lay in the sterile bed, my heart broken open. I believed then that perhaps I was only meant to have one child. Fear wrapped around me like chains, I couldn't imagine enduring this pain again.

The days stretched into years, and though time softened the sharp edges, the questions never fully left me. *Could I have done something differently? Could I have saved my baby?* That little "Baby's First Christmas" sleeper remained tucked away, a sacred symbol of the life we dreamed about but never got to hold.

And yet, life has a way of surprising us. A few short months later, we found ourselves expecting again. This time, it was a son. Karson. If we had carried that second baby to term, we would never have known the gift of him. I believe with all my heart that God knew what we could not, that He had a blessing hidden beyond our heartbreak.

Years later, we were blessed again with another daughter, Kaylee. Our family grew, stitched together with both joy and sorrow, loss and redemption. And still, every now and then, our children talk about the sibling they never met. They wonder aloud what he or she would have been like.

They even speak of Heaven, imagining the day they'll finally meet.

It's been 20 years, yet it feels like yesterday. The pain still flickers at unexpected moments, a quiet ache in my chest. I've always believed it was a little girl we lost. I often wonder what she would have been like, what her laugh would have sounded like, what dreams she would have chased. But when I look at Karson, I am reminded: God knew I needed him.

Our tragedy became the pathway to a blessing we couldn't have imagined. It didn't erase the pain, but it reshaped it into perspective. Life is fragile, fleeting, and immeasurably precious. That loss taught me to cherish every breath, every heartbeat, every hug.

And though our second baby never wore the Christmas sleeper, her existence changed me forever. Through her, I learned that even in loss, God's plan is still laced with love.

Grateful for Rainbows

The first time it happened, it came like a thief: silent, unannounced, merciless. We had barely begun to dream, just a month of shy smiles and whispered prayers, hope fragile as glass. August still burned warm, the air thick with life, and deep within me, something sacred stirred. I didn't even know it yet.

The discovery came in the cruelest way: I was already losing the baby when I learned I was carrying life. It started with a flutter of nausea, a ripple that barely registered, and then the bleeding—wrong, sudden, undeniable. I stood in my bathroom, staring at the faint pink line trembling in my hands. Wonder and heartbreak collided. I whispered a prayer of thanks to the God who gives life, even as my body let go of it. One day, there was a possibility. The next, there was absence.

The pain was sharp and strange, a deep cramping like waves pulling me under. I kept moving through my days because there was no script for this, no way to prepare for becoming a mother and a mourner in a single breath. The grief came later, stealthy and quiet. It slipped into the ordinary: folding laundry, scrolling past baby announcements, standing in church as songs of praise rose around me.

I said little. I tucked it away because I didn't know how to explain the weight of something invisible. Miscarriage belonged to other women's stories, not mine. I was naïve. I believed a positive test was a promise fulfilled. My first child became a memory before they became a heartbeat, and I carried that small ache into every prayer thereafter.

The second loss was different. It tore me wide open.

December was cold, lights twinkling against dark nights, Christmas warming every corner. This time, I knew. My body hummed with life—tender, nauseous, beautifully alive—and my heart soared. I told only my mom, wrapping this tiny soul in secrecy and prayer. "Lord," I begged. "Let this one stay. Please, let this one stay."

Eight weeks passed. Long enough to dream, to picture tiny fingers, to imagine a laugh I'd one day know. And then came the spotting, a hint of blood, a whisper of dread.

The doctor smiled gently, "Probably nothing. Let's check."

The room was dim, the gel cool on my belly. I watched the screen, waiting for music, for the rhythmic thrum of life. But the silence was deafening. "No heartbeat." The words were careful, clinical. Growth had stopped. My baby was gone. They said it was like lightning striking twice. But it didn't feel like lightning. It felt like the ground was giving way.

Snow fell softly as I left the clinic, numb. At home, grief became a storm, sobs breaking through prayers, prayers breaking into cries: "Why, God? Why again?" My Bible lay open but wordless, yet I clung to it like a lifeline.

Then came the choices, cold, impossible: Awake or asleep? Hospital or home? Pill or a procedure? No one prepared me for what those words meant. No one told me that losing a baby at home would feel like labor, that pain would curl me inward, that blood would seem endless. And no one told me that I would hold my baby in the palm of my hand; tiny, real, impossibly precious.

We buried that little one in the backyard. My husband and I wrote a letter, placed it with flower petals and a soft swaddle in a small box. I wrote words with shaking hands: "I love you. I wanted you. I will see you again." As the earth closed over that tiny grave, Heaven felt unbearably close.

Faith grew harder then. Some days, prayer was nothing but silence. Other days, it was a single phrase whispered to the sky, "Lord, I don't understand." I met God in my tears, in therapy rooms where I confessed my shame: I feel broken. I feel abandoned. I feel less.

Yet somehow, light slipped in, friends who brought meals, scripture that felt like balm, a husband who held me steady when I crumbled.

Loss reshaped me. It made me gentler and fiercer, softer and stronger. It carved spaces in me for compassion I didn't know I could hold. It taught me to fight, to search, to knock on Heaven's door with trembling but persistent hands.

And then, July came. My son's arrival was chaos: doctors shouting, a knotted cord, forceps, alarms. But then he cried. Loud and defiant, pink and alive. Joy roared back into my world.

Even now, holding him, I feel the echo of the two who came before. My rainbow baby fills my arms, but the others live in my heart. They are stitched into my soul, reminders that love and loss can coexist, that faith can be bruised and still breathe.

One day, I'll tell my son about his siblings in heaven. I'll tell him that before he came, I learned to hope fiercely, to ache deeply, to trust God even in the dark. And I'll tell him this: His siblings taught me that God's goodness isn't measured by outcomes, but by the way He holds us, even when our hands are empty.

Emmy Day

I will never forget the first moment I saw those two pink lines appear on the test. After years of battling infertility, of blood draws, injections, tears, and silent prayers whispered into the dark, this was the moment I had dreamed of. My hands shook. My heart raced. I could barely breathe. It felt as though the universe had finally handed me the miracle I had begged for.

But after years of disappointment, joy was tangled with fear. At every early appointment, I held my breath, bracing for bad news, whispering promises to a child I hadn't yet met.

Then came the day that changed everything. I was nearly ready to "graduate" from my fertility clinic to my OB's office, a milestone that felt like stepping into the sunlight. The ultrasound room was dim, the screen glowing softly against the wall. I watched the tech move the wand, my chest tightening as the minutes stretched longer.

When the doctor walked in, her smile was wide and her voice steady. "There are two babies."

My mind spun. Two? My embryo had split! We were having identical twin girls. Tears blurred my vision. I couldn't stop smiling. Just weeks earlier I had told friends that I had a feeling. Something inside me knew there were two souls. It seemed my mama's intuition was right. After all we'd been through, not one but two miracles were growing inside me.

But joy rarely travels a straight line.

In the weeks that followed, I learned the shape of fear in a new way. Bleeding started early and became a near-daily rhythm. Every trip to the bathroom sent my heart racing. Every cramp felt like a cliff edge. For weeks, I lived in quiet dread, half expecting to lose them at any moment. At 15 weeks, the bleeding finally stopped, and I let out a cautious breath. A week later, it was stolen from me.

At our early anatomy scan, the air shifted as soon as the tech grew silent. The doctor's voice was calm but heavy: twin-to-twin transfusion syndrome. One baby, our sweet Emmy, was struggling. Her blood flow was reversing.

"There are options," they said. "Laser ablation surgery could give them a chance."

"Can it work?" I asked, desperate, clinging to any thread.

"There's a chance," they said.

So at 17 weeks, I laid on an operating table, the sterile lights harsh above me, my heart beating so loudly I was sure they could hear it. I prayed through every second. When the surgery ended, they told me there were still two heartbeats. Relief washed over me like sunlight after a storm.

But the storm wasn't over.

The next morning, they wheeled me to the ultrasound room. My body felt heavy with exhaustion, but my mind was electric with prayer. As the probe pressed against my belly, I searched the screen. I had learned what a heartbeat looked like by then, and I saw only one. Mollie's heart was strong. Emmy's had silenced.

The room blurred. The sobs came fast and uncontrollable. My baby girl was gone.

We went home that day carrying both grief and hope. Mollie still growing, Emmy now a memory. But barely a day later, I began to bleed again, fluid leaking that no mother ever wants to see. At the hospital, the words stung like bullets: My sac had ruptured. Labor could begin at any moment. The pregnancy might be over.

But somehow, it wasn't.

I refused to let hope die. I turned to the community, Facebook groups, and other mamas who had lived through the impossible. They taught me what to ask, how to fight, what protocols could buy Mollie more time. For 17 weeks, I lived on a tightrope of faith and medicine. Eleven of those weeks were spent in a hospital bed, the walls becoming both my cage and my sanctuary.

On May 30, 2019, after all the prayers, all the tears, all the quiet courage I didn't know I had, Mollie was born. She was tiny, impossibly small, but fierce. I swear I felt Emmy there with us, her presence like a whisper in the room. I believe she gave her sister strength to make it earthside.

Mollie is now the bright star of our lives, a daily reminder of perseverance and grace. Emmy lives with us too—in memory, in love, in the quiet spaces. Every year we honor her with "Emmy Day," inviting friends and family to do a random act of kindness in her name. Mollie asks about her sister often, if they would look alike, laugh alike. She talks to Emmy as if she knows her, and I believe, in a very special way, they are still connected.

When I think back to those endless weeks on bedrest, I remember the affirmations I whispered daily. The letters I wrote to Mollie. The necklace I now wear with both their names engraved, a weight on my heart and around my neck. Mollie has one too. When she sees a rainbow, she points and says, "That's Emmy."

To every mother who has carried both hope and heartbreak, you are not alone. Your baby's memory lives in you. Your grief and your joy can coexist. Tell your story. Honor your child because even the shortest lives can leave the deepest love behind.

Luke's Story

There are some stories we don't choose, but they shape us all the same. This one shaped me. And if you're reading it, maybe, in some way, it has something to say to you too.

When I first found out I was pregnant, it felt like the air shifted around me. I had known in my heart for weeks, quietly certain before the test confirmed it, but it still took nearly two weeks past my missed cycle for the word *pregnant* to finally appear. I remember standing in the bathroom, the test trembling in my hands, my heart pounding so loud I could hear it in my ears. At that moment, all I could think about was who this little soul would become. I whispered, *This is it. We're having a baby.*

From that moment, I began to imagine who this tiny soul might become. The thought of holding him someday filled me with a kind of hope I'd never known before. We were absolutely ecstatic.

Those first weeks carried me on a tide of exhaustion. I could fall asleep almost anywhere, but I didn't mind. Fatigue was a small price for the miracle of life growing inside me. When we finally began sharing the news with our closest friends and family at 12 weeks, the joy doubled. Every time I said the words *I'm pregnant*, the reality grew more solid, more beautiful.

At our 20-week anatomy scan, we watched as the doctor pointed out every perfect detail, from his fingers to the steady beat of his heart. I couldn't stop staring at the screen, memorizing the way his little body shifted and turned. That moment lives inside me still, a reminder of how much wonder can be held in a single heartbeat.

We decided to keep the baby's gender a surprise, wanting to wait until the day of delivery for the great unveiling. In the meantime, we celebrated with a babymoon to Sedona and Scottsdale, walking red rock trails and lingering over dinners, savoring those last days of just us before parenthood began. I was nearly 22 weeks along, and everything felt alive with possibility.

Then the cramping started. At first, I brushed it aside, blaming the food I'd been indulging in or the busy days of travel. But the pain sharpened, and when the bleeding began, fear settled deep in my chest. I knew. I knew something was terribly wrong.

On Christmas Eve, we rushed to the hospital. The brightness of the triage lights, the urgent glances between nurses, the way no one could quite meet my eyes all told me more than their words could. Fear pressed down on me like a weight I couldn't push off. They tried to stop the labor, tried to save him, tried everything. But it wasn't enough.

In the earliest hours of Christmas morning, I delivered my son. Luke.

There is no way to describe the silence of a room where a baby should be crying but isn't. No words for the weight of holding him, saying both hello and goodbye in the same breath. There is only an aching void. We held him. We kissed him. We said goodbye. The hospital staff gave us a box with his blanket, tiny photographs, and hospital band. I clutched that box like it contained his entire existence, because in some ways, it did.

Not only did we lose our son, but we were across the country from family, aching to be home, trying to figure out how to grieve and travel all at once. The grief was so raw, so unrelenting, it felt like trying to breathe underwater.

Two weeks later, when I thought I couldn't break any further, I hemorrhaged. The emergency D&C was not just another physical trauma, it quietly stole even more from me. Scar tissue filled my womb, and months later I was diagnosed with Asherman's Syndrome, a rare condition where scar tissue forms in the uterus, blocking the normal shedding of the uterine lining. Procedure after procedure, surgery after surgery, we tried to restore what was lost. We tried Intra-Uterine Inseminations (IUIs.). We tried hope. We tried to coax my body into holding life again, but it would not. The truth came slowly, then all at once: My body would not carry another child, and I would need a surrogate to continue my journey.

That truth nearly shattered me. It wasn't just the loss of Luke, it was the loss of the future I had built in my mind, the sound of children's laughter in our home, the growing family I dreamed of. I had to grieve Luke, and then grieve the future I believed was mine.

My husband and I clung to each other, holding fast against the storm. We sought counseling, found words for our sorrow, learned how to breathe through waves of pain.

Although grief has never loosened its grip entirely, over time we have learned how to live inside the ache of it.

Now, as Luke's ninth birthday draws near, I can say this: The pain has not disappeared, and it never will. But I have learned how to carry it. It has become a part of me, woven into who I am. Love still exists. I have built a life where both grief and happiness stand side by side, one never erasing the other.

Luke's story is written into who I am. He may not have stayed, but he shaped me, even in his short time. He made me a mother. And he will always, *always* be part of who I am.

A Date Shared

I was only 18, still half a child myself, when I lost my first baby. My life was knotted up in the intensity of young love, the kind that keeps pulling you back even when you think you've walked away for good. He was my first love, my high school sweetheart, and though our relationship was as unsteady as the ground in springtime, I clung to it.

I still remember the sterile chill of the gynecologist's office, the way the paper gown crackled every time I shifted on the table. My regular doctor had sent me there for a biopsy after an abnormal pap smear. I was already nervous, heart fluttering, palms damp, but underneath it all, there was this quiet whisper in my body: *What if I'm pregnant?* We had had an accident, a broken condom, and although my period hadn't come yet, my breasts ached, my body felt different, almost tender with possibility.

I asked for a test, my voice a little shaky, more like a plea than a request. But the doctor waved it off. No need. It won't matter. Even if you were pregnant, this won't hurt anything. Those words would echo in my head for years.

I lay there under the fluorescent light while the biopsy tool pinched at me, sharp and foreign. A discomfort that felt wrong. I asked again. "Shouldn't we test?" But my words were brushed aside. When it was over, I went home, trying to convince myself I was overreacting.

The next day, my period came, or what I thought was my period. Only it wasn't right. The cramps were deeper, twisting me in two. The blood was darker, nearly black, heavy with something ominous. And then, in the bathroom, I heard it, a small pop into the toilet. I leaned over, frozen, and there it was: a small sac, tangled tissue. Life that had been, and now was not.

I was just a teenager, working at Blockbuster, still living under my parents' roof. They didn't even know I had been with anyone. In our religious home, sex before marriage wasn't just forbidden, it was unspeakable. My secret pressed down on me like a stone. So I did the only thing I knew to do, I flushed. And the sound of it haunted me. I flushed my baby down the toilet.

My doctor later confirmed what my body already knew. A miscarriage. She told me to watch for fever and infection, to call if things got worse. And things did get worse. I ended up in the hospital, shaking with fever, but they told me I'd be fine. Physically, at least.

Emotionally, I was unraveling. At the same time, I had been babysitting a little boy, a child neglected by his parents. I would wash him, feed him, hold him, try to give him the tenderness he was missing at home. After my miscarriage, though, the thought of holding him shredded me. I told his parents I couldn't take him one night, and they cut me off completely. Another loss stacked on top of the first.

Then came the biopsy results: precancerous cells. I had to return to the very doctor who had ignored my pleas for a pregnancy test. I had to lie again on that cold table, legs in stirrups, while they froze my cervix raw. They didn't pause to let me heal, didn't acknowledge that I had just miscarried. One nurse even said, "It's a blessing. You're only eighteen. You had no right to a baby anyway."

I wanted to scream: It wasn't your decision! It was mine! But instead, I just screamed from the pain as they burned me, my voice echoing all the way to the waiting room where my friend sat, helpless.

I carried that grief like a shadow, replaying the what-ifs, the could-have-beens, the ache of being so young, so alone, with no one to tell, no parents I could confide in, no arms to fall into. Just shame and silence in the Bible Belt, where sin was spoken louder than sorrow.

And yet, life moved forward. My boyfriend and I mended things and married not long after. I never went back on birth control. Eventually, I became pregnant again. This time, joy poured into me like sunlight. And when the doctor told me the due date, I froze. It was the same day I had miscarried, only two years later. It was as if life itself was trying to write a new story across the scar of the old one.

That first loss has never left me. It shaped me before I even knew how to carry grief. It taught me what silence can do to a heart. And though I was only 18, I knew this: No one else could decide the worth of my child or the weight of my love.

The Box Beside My Brother

By the time I reached my fifth miscarriage, I had already carried the weight of so many losses that each new pregnancy felt like balancing hope on a trembling wire. But this time was supposed to be different. Doctors had finally discovered the parathyroid tumor that had been poisoning my body for years, pushing calcium to dangerous levels in my blood. They told me it might have been the silent culprit behind my miscarriages. With the tumor gone, my body finally felt like it might be safe for new life. So when I saw those two lines, my heart dared to hope again. This baby would be the one, a younger sibling for Trace and my other two.

I can still remember how small he was then, barely toddling around, not yet two. The thought of him with a little brother or sister filled me with a warmth that reached deeper than words.

But that warmth soon turned to worry. My first blood test came back with numbers too low. The nurse tried to reassure me, told me it was early, that sometimes levels took time. I clung to that. We went back again, then again. Each time the numbers rose, but not enough, not in the steady rhythm of a healthy pregnancy. It was a cruel tease, this upward climb that always fell short of the line we needed.

Finally, the doctor sat me down. His words were blunt, without pause for the fragile hope I was holding: "The pregnancy isn't viable. We need to intervene." He prescribed a pill, a chemotherapy drug, he explained, harsh enough to dissolve the tissue, to clear what my body wouldn't. He spoke as if it were simple, clinical. But to me it was unbearable. I had been through D&Cs before, but this, swallowing poison to end the life inside me, felt like betrayal.

I begged for an ultrasound. He told me it wasn't necessary, that there would be nothing to see. But I couldn't accept that. I needed proof. Finally, annoyed, he sent me down the street to radiology.

And there it was: Nothing. A blank screen, no heartbeat, no flicker. Empty. I walked back, my chest hollow, still whispering the same protest. *Maybe it's just too early. Maybe the baby's too small to see.* But his words crushed it: *Baby girl, it's not viable. I wouldn't lie to you.*

I left with the pill. And I broke.

By then, grief had seeped into every corner of me. This was my fifth loss. The depression that had followed the others now pulled me under in ways I could no longer resist. I drank too much, moved through my days like a ghost, detached from my children, my husband, my own body. One night, I slid into the bathtub with a bottle and a notebook. The room smelled of warm water and sharp alcohol. Words spilled across the page, confessions I couldn't say out loud. *I don't want to be here anymore. I can't carry this pain.*

I wasn't planning to end my life, but the thought of not living pressed so close it blurred the line. I fell asleep in the water, notebook open on the edge. My husband found me there, shook me awake, terror in his eyes, convinced he'd lost me too. I told him I hadn't done anything, but the truth was clear, I was drowning in my own grief.

We knew then something had to change. I needed to honor the children I had lost, to give them a resting place even if my body hadn't. I found a small wooden box, simple but beautiful, and filled it with tokens of their brief existence: ultrasound pictures, the "baby on board" sign I'd once used to surprise my husband, tiny rattles, a scrap of baby blanket soft against my fingertips. Even tissue from this last miscarriage, because it was all I had left of that child.

My brother had died before I was old enough to remember him, but I always felt tethered to him. So I took the box to his grave, shovel in hand. Kneeling by the cool stone, I dug into the earth at his side and laid the box in, whispering through tears: *Take care of them for me until I can be with them again.* Then I covered it, letting the soil fall over the weight of my five babies, leaving them safe with their uncle.

That act gave me a strange kind of peace, but it also forced me to face the end. I was nearing 38, and we made a decision: If I wasn't pregnant by my birthday, we would stop trying. It was time to step out of the cycle of hope and devastation.

Those nine months became my grieving space, my way of preparing for goodbye. By the time my birthday came, and I wasn't pregnant, I felt ready. I looked at my three beautiful living children and felt gratitude bloom where longing once lived. My husband scheduled a vasectomy. We were done.

Then life with its mischievous twists reminded me I was never truly in control. One month later, after a single, ordinary night together, I found myself holding a dollar-store pregnancy test with shaking hands. Positive. My daughter knew instantly. She teased me that the only reason I ever stopped at Dollar General was for those tests.

But instead of joy, what rushed in was fear. We had already said goodbye. We had already accepted an ending. This new beginning felt fragile, edged with dread. Every day of that pregnancy was a cautious breath, waiting for loss to find me again. But the weeks passed, the trimesters shifted, and finally hope held steady. At Christmas, we opened a small, wrapped package that held the gender results: a baby girl.

And when she came, with her brown hair and green eyes, I couldn't help but laugh at the prayer I had whispered to God. He had answered, not in the way I expected, but in a way that stitched my story back together with grace I didn't deserve.

Even now, I visit my brother's grave, where my five little ones rest beneath the soil. My father's ashes are there too, scattered at his request, so he could watch over them. Sometimes I stand there, tracing their names in my mind, knowing they are cared for, knowing I will see them again one day. Until then, I carry them with me always in the quiet places of my heart.

When Silence Speaks

I was just 19, barely stepping into adulthood, when I saw those two pink lines. My hands trembled as I held the test, the weight of it sinking in slowly. *Nervous.* That was the first word that settled over me. Nervous to tell my parents, nervous because I was still living at home, nervous because my life felt like it was only just beginning.

But beneath the nerves, excitement hummed. Brandon and I had been together for years, high school sweethearts who had grown up alongside one another. We didn't have our careers figured out. We didn't have much mapped out at all, but in that moment, becoming parents felt like the right next step, wild and unexpected as it was.

The nerves of telling our parents melted quicker than I expected. Their faces softened, and their words wrapped around us with encouragement. And soon, that nervous energy shifted into a quiet joy. I bought prenatal vitamins, tucked them into my nightstand, and felt like I was stepping into a new version of myself.

The first checkup went well, nothing remarkable, but reassuring enough. It was still so early, just a few weeks in, but everything looked fine. We left the office smiling, Brandon squeezing my hand, the future stretching out before us.

The second appointment, though, the one where we were supposed to hear the heartbeat, everything changed. I remember lying there, the cool gel on my stomach, the ultrasound wand moving slowly. The technician's silence was heavy, filling the room like smoke. Brandon and I looked at the screen, waiting, searching for that flicker, that sound, that proof of life.

But the longer it went on, the quieter it became, not just in the room, but also in my heart. The air dimmed, as if the light itself had pulled back. The tech excused herself, came back with the doctor. They tried again. And then came the words no new parent ever wants to hear: "I'm so sorry... there's no heartbeat."

We sat in stunned silence, the words pressing down on us. We didn't cry at first. We just froze, holding hands, staring at the floor, trying to understand how joy could dissolve into grief so quickly.

That evening, when Brandon's mom came home from work, we stood on the stairs, tears already burning in our eyes. She looked at us once and knew something was wrong. When we whispered, "There was no heartbeat," she rushed forward, gathering us into her arms. We all cried together, our grief spilling over in waves.

Telling my parents was just as hard. Later, my mom told me how deeply it hurt her, not just for the baby we lost but for the pain of watching her own daughter suffer.

Because I was 12 weeks along, my doctor recommended a D&C. I remember sitting with that decision, the strangeness of it, surgery to remove the baby I had just begun to dream of. Fear and grief tangled together, but I knew it was necessary. Both our families showed up that day, standing quietly in the hospital as if their presence alone could carry me through.

The procedure was quick, outpatient. My body was exhausted and nauseated afterward, and the day itself was a blur. But the emotional ache lingered far longer, the ache of empty hands, of dreams paused before they could take shape.

That was April of 2014. Just six months later, in October, we discovered we were expecting again. This time, it was our daughter, Cora, our joy, our light, our living reminder of resilience. She's 10 now, with a laugh that fills rooms and a presence that heals places in me I didn't know were still broken.

But even in the fullness of her life and her brothers, I carry the memory of the one who came before them, the heartbeat I never heard, the baby I never got to hold. I believe one day I will. Until then, I carry them all: the child I lost, and the two who turned my grief into something holy.

The Loss That Bound Us

On August 9, 2015, my world shifted. My momom, my grandmother, my anchor, passed away, and her absence cracked our family open in ways we weren't ready for. She had always been the center of our world, the one we loved beyond measure. That day, in the blur of grief, I called the only person who could hold me steady: my boyfriend, now my husband.

He was in the Air Force, stationed in South Carolina, and for years our relationship had been lived in fragments, visits once a month, long-distance calls, stolen weekends. He caught an emergency flight to be with me and was by my side in those raw hours of loss. That same night, the night we lost her, we created life.

It wasn't planned. I was on the pill. He used protection. Life was busy, chaotic. I was a full-time college student, juggling a house full of roommates, an internship, and a part-time job. He was chasing a military career. A baby was not in our plans.

The first month, I bled lightly and thought it was my period, not knowing it was implantation. By the third month, when no period came, I bought a test. Alone in the bathroom, I watched blue lines appear, my hands trembling, tears spilling, not of joy, but of anxiety. How could I tell him? How could I tell my parents?

When I finally called, his voice was steady but tight. He was scared too, but he promised: We'll get through this together. And so we made a plan. He would fly up, help me pack, break the news to my roommates, then we'd drive downstate to face my family before heading back to South Carolina. I transferred my degree online, applied for jobs near the base.

We were moving pieces into place, but neither of us could savor the news. There was no joyful announcement, no glowing anticipation, only the heavy knowledge that our families wouldn't support us if we stayed together without marriage.

In quiet moments, we tried to comfort ourselves. Maybe, we said, this baby was Momom's way of carrying on, of leaving a piece of her with us. She had loved him so much. That thought was enough to spark hope, even laughter, between us.

But at 19 weeks, hope unraveled.

It began with cramps, sharp and growing. By the next day, I was bleeding and vomiting. By day three, I couldn't leave the toilet. Dehydrated, weak, terrified, I finally let a roommate drive me, not to the ER, but to the women's maternity home. She was hurt, blindsided that I hadn't shared my pregnancy, and that fracture cost us our friendship.

Inside the clinic, I labored unmedicated. The nurse pressed my shoulders down, whispering, "It's okay. It'll all be over soon." Her words stung. I didn't want it to be over, not like this. And yet, it was. I delivered our stillborn, empty-handed and broken.

In the fog of grief, I chose to donate our baby to science. I hoped, if anything, that our loss could protect another woman from facing the same pain. We never gave a name.

When I called him my boyfriend, his sobs met mine through the static of the phone. We grieved, but beneath it was something even heavier, guilt. Relief had been tangled in our sorrow. Relief that the timing, the circumstances, the fear of disappointing our families were gone. That guilt haunted us both.

I cried for days. Anger welled up when he didn't talk about it unless I brought it up. I needed to hear his heart, his pain, his words. But he stayed silent, carrying his grief alone. I spiraled, tormented by thoughts that my relief had damned me, that I was selfish, greedy, unworthy of Heaven, unworthy of meeting our baby again. He begged me not to believe it, but the guilt cut us both deep.

We carried on because we had to. I went to class, clocked into work, held myself together while unraveling inside. He deployed again and again, gone for months at a time. We didn't see each other until two months after the loss. That reunion broke something open. In his arms, for the first time since the miscarriage, I slept without terrors. When the nightmares came, they lessened with him beside me.

Life kept us apart except for monthly visits through 2016, then an overseas stationing through 2017. But that one weekend together taught us something essential: We could survive this. We could hold grief and love in the same hands. We could dream of children again, not as replacements, but as blessings born of endurance.

We married in June 2020. Our son was born in June 2023. Even now, there are nights when the "what ifs" creep in, when we wonder who our baby would have been. My pregnancy with our son was shadowed by fear, my anxiety climbing with every milestone. The night terrors returned. But holding him now, healthy, laughing, full of light, I know grief and gratitude can live side by side.

Loss taught us gratitude. It carved out space for compassion. It bound us together in a way nothing else could. Although another child may fill our arms, none will ever replace the one we lost. That baby remains with us, unseen but never forgotten, a part of our family forever.

Our First Hello Was Goodbye

I think it was around 2011 when we first learned my brother was going to be a father. He was barely out of high school, maybe even still in it, and his girlfriend was the same, both of them hovering around 17, standing on the edge of adulthood with the weight of everything already pressing down on them.

Our family didn't know about the pregnancy until she was four or five months along. My mom had suspected it, noticing the subtle changes: the gentle rounding of her belly, the softening of her face, the way her hands rested lightly, protectively, over a life no one else could see yet.

I was living in Florida then, far from Ohio, and every mile felt like a wall I couldn't climb. I tried to be present in small ways, phone calls that lasted too long, sometimes awkward, sometimes filled with nervous laughter. Often, I asked her to put the phone on her belly. I wanted my voice to reach my niece, to vibrate against her skin, to whisper that she was already loved. The thought of being an aunt in name only haunted me. What if she never felt me? What if I was just a distant echo, someone she recognized but never truly knew?

Before the pregnancy, I had resented this girl, my brother's girlfriend. I thought she distracted him, pulled him away from his life, from his future. But the moment I learned a baby was coming, all of that melted away. Every judgment, every irritation was gone. My heart only wanted to know my niece, to find my place in her life, even from afar.

But then, just as we began imagining her, the sound of her laughter, the curve of her little hands, the tilt of her head, everything changed. Something went wrong. A knot in the umbilical cord. A cruel twist of fate that cut off her oxygen. My brother and his girlfriend rushed to the hospital with panic choking them, but there was nothing anyone could do. She was delivered, perfectly formed, utterly still.

I drove 13 hours straight, my hands gripping the wheel so tightly my knuckles whitened, the night stretching endlessly before me, punctuated only by the blur of headlights on asphalt. When I arrived at the hospital, the first thing that hit me was the smell: antiseptic sharp in the air, mixed with the faint sweetness of baby lotion, a scent that should have meant life but here carried only absence. The low hum of monitors, the shuffle of nurses' shoes against linoleum, it all pressed down, heavy and surreal.

Then I saw her. They were holding her. I remember the way the fluorescent lights caught her skin, pale and creamy with bruises of violet in the creases, her lips deep purple, curling slightly as if to smile but unable. She was impossibly small, delicate as porcelain, fragile enough to disappear if I looked away. In another context, she might have seemed beautiful. Here, every shade, every line, was a mark of loss.

I passed her from arm to arm with my family, our movements slow, reverent. My mother's hands trembled as she brushed a finger over her tiny cheek. My brother's face was blank, hollow-eyed, as if he were watching through a fog. I wanted to cry out, to scream, to shake the unfairness from the walls. But instead, we moved quietly, afraid that any sound might shatter this fragile, impossible moment.

Every small gesture was magnified: the brush of a hand over her head, the gentle shift of her tiny body in our arms, the collective intake of breath whenever we passed her between us. The room was thick with unspoken grief, eyes locking for a fraction of a second, then darting away; hands resting on each other's shoulders, offering contact that said "we are here, together" without words.

For days, the hospital staff would return her in a small cooler box when asked. My brother, dazed, hollow, whispered, "Why isn't she in the nursery? Why does she have to be kept like this in the morgue?" His voice broke me, splintered me in ways I didn't know I could feel. I could see the panic, the fear, the unbearable question of how to continue when the world had just stopped.

I had to be the one to speak, to guide them to the impossible step of letting her go before her body changed, before the fleeting perfection we held slipped into a form we couldn't bear to see.

I can still feel her weight in my arms, a weight so light it could have been imagined, yet so full of presence. I remember the faint warmth of her skin, the fragile pulse of existence that somehow lingered after life had left, the smell of baby lotion and hospital air mingling in a way that burned into my memory. I wonder endlessly what she might have been like. Would she have had her mother's quiet smile, the one that made strangers pause? My brother's restless energy, a spark that could never sit still? Sometimes I see her younger brother and feel a stabbing ache, imagining the laughter that might have been and the banter that we never got to hear.

What lingers most, the thing that pierces quietly in every ordinary moment, is the awkwardness of naming them as parents. Calling them mom and dad when their child never left the hospital walls feels both right and impossible. Was it cruel not to? Did my silence add another layer to their grief, a quiet exclusion that felt necessary, protective, but also like betrayal? These questions return in the small, ordinary moments: the hum of a refrigerator, the flicker of light across a wall, the whisper of wind through trees. Grief doesn't end. It reshapes itself, a shadow tethered to love, a constant reminder that some hellos end in goodbyes.

Twice Broken, Once Redeemed

Before I ever saw two pink lines on a test, I had already made peace with the idea that motherhood might never come the way I'd dreamed. Years earlier, at just 22, I'd faced ovarian cancer. The treatments had saved my ovaries, but the doctors were blunt: The medications might not work, and even if they did, they could send me spiraling into early menopause. For years after, every missed cycle, every shift in my body, I told myself it was just that, the slow fading out of possibility. By the time I was 37, I had convinced myself I would adopt if I ever wanted children.

So when my period began to change, I thought nothing of it. *Menopause,* I told myself. Another door closed, quietly. My employee, sharp-eyed and unfiltered, cut straight through my denial. "Go buy a pregnancy test," she said one morning, exasperated. "You're being mean."

I laughed it off, shaking my head. No. I wasn't doing that to myself again. I had endured too many months of waiting, too many years of hope knotted into a single line that never came. With my husband before, David, it had always been the same outcome. One line. Empty. Loss without ever having been. "No," I told her. "It's menopause. I'll be fine."

Three days later, she handed me a test anyway. I remember locking myself in the bathroom, the stick trembling in my hand, and then watching, heart pounding, as not one but two pink lines appeared. My knees buckled. I sobbed. Surely it had to be wrong. After so many years of no, how could this be yes? I called the doctor that very day. When she confirmed it, "You're pregnant," the words cracked something open in me. Joy, fear, disbelief, grief for all the years before, it all came rushing at once.

But at seven weeks, I started to bleed. Panic surged like fire in my chest as I sat in the sterile office, the paper gown crinkling beneath me. The doctor's words were detached, clinical. "There's nothing we can do. We'll have to wait and let it run its course."

I wanted to scream, to demand more, but everywhere I turned I felt judged, dismissed. Nurses spoke to me like I should have known what to expect. How could I? It was my first time ever being pregnant. And then, just like that, I wasn't.

The loss hit me harder than anything I could have imagined. My body betrayed me, hormones crashing all at once, leaving me hollow and unstable. One afternoon, panic swallowed me whole. My heart raced; my vision blurred. I lost control of my car, slammed into a wall head-on, and walked away without a scratch. I was physically unharmed, but inside, I total wreckage. I closed myself off from everyone, drowning in silence.

When I became pregnant again, I told no one. At four weeks, I miscarried quietly at work, slipped back into my duties as if nothing had happened. I carried that loss alone, invisible to the world.

A year later, I thought I had found love again. But grief had made me cautious, almost defensive. Every time ovulation came near, I found excuses to stay away. My partner grew angry, impatient. I couldn't tell him the truth: that the idea of another loss terrified me more than loneliness ever could. But fate, or perhaps God, had other plans. That month, my body ovulated twice. Despite my careful avoidance, life slipped in anyway.

My employee knew before I did. I cried when I found out. I wasn't ready. I had just broken away from a man whose cruelty lingered in every corner of my life. I couldn't imagine carrying another loss on top of that. This time, I waited until 16 weeks to tell anyone.

But fear followed me. My ex's stalking, his harassment pushed me to the edge, and one day, the bleeding began again. My stomach dropped. Not again. Please, not again. I braced myself for goodbye. But when I went to the doctor, they found him still there, hanging on. Strong. Twice I bled, twice I thought I would lose him, but each time he held on.

And then I met the doctor who changed everything. He refused to dismiss me. He listened. He acted. He cared. He fought for this little one with me as if my baby's life was as sacred to him as it was to me. And slowly, impossibly, the fear began to give way to hope.

Zurich. My miracle. My rainbow. Born just two weeks before my 39th birthday, he arrived not as fragile as I feared, but fierce, strong, defiant. My double rainbow baby. The child who said to me, even before he could speak, "No, Mama. Not this time. I'll be strong enough for the both of us." And he was. He still is.

Born to Defy the Odds

I was born a triplet in 1970, but I came into the world already marked by loss. The third baby, my sibling, never took a breath. I survived, though barely, at just one and a half pounds of fragile, uncertain life. The doctors lined my parents' days with predictions, each one a deadline I wasn't supposed to cross. She won't live past infancy. She won't walk. She won't reach puberty. She'll never carry children of her own. Every milestone I reached was defiance, every birthday a quiet rebellion.

Puberty came late. I was 15 before my body caught up, and even then, complications wove themselves into my story. At 18, just months after losing my virginity, I had my first miscarriage. By 24, I had lost seven babies across six pregnancies with my first husband. The last was the hardest: twins, carried until six months, gone too soon.

Eventually, doctors found the reasons behind the heartbreak: a heart-shaped uterus, one fallopian tube clogged. My body had its own strange rhythm. Sometimes the ovary on the blocked side would release an egg, and against all odds, it would travel across to the open tube. Some months, there were two eggs ready. I was fertile, sometimes wildly so, yet fertility meant nothing when my body couldn't hold on to the lives it created.

And then, I met my second husband. The very first time we were together, I became pregnant. History had taught me to brace myself for loss, and for months I lived on edge, waiting for the familiar ending. But that pregnancy was different. I didn't even realize I was pregnant until

85

nearly five months had passed. At six months, labor came early, and fear surged again. Doctors stopped it, but I spent the rest of the pregnancy on bedrest and Brethine, a medicine that made my muscles twitch with contractions so that my uterus wouldn't.

At 42½ weeks, against every prediction, every past heartbreak, I gave birth to a healthy 7-pound, 3-ounce girl. She was more than my daughter; she was proof that sometimes miracles choose the most broken places to bloom. Even now, when I look at her grown and thriving, I see all the "nevers" I was told reflected back at me as living, breathing yeses.

Six months later, I got another surprise. My son. A double-condom baby, as if fate itself insisted he was meant to be here. Again, I went into early labor, and again bedrest and Brethine carried me through. At 42½ weeks, he arrived, 8 pounds, 2 ounces of stubborn, thriving life. Today, when I watch him laugh or see him carve out his own path in the world, I still marvel at the impossibility of his existence.

When they circumcised him, I had my tubal ligation. My doctor was firm: My body couldn't survive another pregnancy. I listened, grateful for the two miracles I had been entrusted with, but my story wasn't finished yet.

In 2001, I was formally diagnosed with endometriosis, although I had lived with it since I was a teenager, long before the condition had a name. Surgeries confirmed it again and again. Because of the disease, my tubal grew back, and over the next 15 years, I lost another 12 to 15 pregnancies. Eight of them ended with a D&C. Each loss added to the scar tissue inside me, and each surgery aggravated the disease further. Anesthesia was dangerous too, and I was allergic to acetaminophen. Every procedure was a risk I might not come back from.

Menopause came in my late thirties, earlier than most, and in a way, it was a relief. I stepped onto the backside of the disease, into remission after four decades of battling it. The war inside my body finally quieted.

I buried only two of my babies. The rest remain with me in memory, in spirit, in the lessons they left behind. But I was blessed to bring two children earthside, both carried not just to term but beyond. They are the greatest work of my life, the proof that love and stubborn hope can bend fate.

Losing so many babies didn't break me. It made me strong enough to love my children deeper, fiercer. It gave me wisdom to teach them, lessons born from pain but shaped into love. Each little life, whether it breathed or not, left me with something. A blessing. A skill. A piece of strength.

Now when I gather with my children, when I hear their voices or see them laugh, I feel the presence of all the others too. They live in the patience I taught, in the tenderness I give, in the grit I passed down.

I somehow took those tragedies and turned them into miracles.

We Are *not* Broken

Ever since I was a little girl I knew one title would sit right on me: Mother. Other things, careers, college majors, plans, floated past like stray clouds. I tried them on, and they never fit. But I could see myself clear as daylight with a baby in my arms: tender mornings, a name whispered at night, my whole purpose shaped into tiny fingers and the weight of a life that needed me.

After graduation, I gave seven years to a man who kept me close but never promised forever. I stayed because I thought babies would make it honest, that somehow, if I birthed what I'd always wanted, my life would be complete. It wasn't. When I left at 26, I crossed the country with nothing but a duffel bag and bruised hope. I started over, completely alone.

I found purpose in caregiving. As a Certified Nursing Assistant, I smelled antiseptic and warm lotion, heard the steady beeps of monitors and the rasp of old breaths. Helping people filled some hollow place within me. Then the Covid-19 pandemic came and spread hopelessness into every hallway I walked. I watched bodies shrink behind curtains, hope fade, and helplessness settled in my gut.

As I traveled alone between facilities, surrounded by suffering I couldn't fix, the darkness crept in. Who would miss me if I vanished? I was alone with no husband beside me, no children's laughter in the house, not even the comfort of my dog at my feet. It was as if everything I had prayed for, every picture I'd painted of my future, had dissolved into something I could see but never hold.

I didn't let myself fall though. Not yet. If I couldn't trust a man to protect me without owning me, I would be the protector of my own life. If I couldn't have children alone, I would build purpose instead. I decided to start a service business, my Plan B. It was something I could own, something that let me breathe. Couch surfing, late-night shifts, and bad dates filled the gaps of my days, and slowly, the business grew. I worked a full-time job by day and built my dream by night. Gradually, Plan B became steadier than the men I'd met.

Then one day, Hardy appeared at work. I said no to him at first, too busy, too fragile to let someone in. He persisted. He offered to help me on a job and stayed unpaid just to be near me. I let him in, and two weeks later, everything shifted. The Blox- a highly competitive entrepreneur bootcamp that's filmed as a reality TV show accepted me, I earned a promotion, and I moved into a little two-bedroom house with a big yard for my dogs and a garage for my business. Clients came without effort. I began training an employee. For the first time in a long time, I felt in control. Happy.

Fast forward to February 2025. I was a month shy of 30. I told myself 30 would be my year!

The night before I left for The Blox, Hardy and I said goodbye in the most intimate of ways. The week away on The Blox was one of the best of my life. I learned, laughed, and felt like I belonged. I didn't know it then, but I was already carrying life inside me.

Two weeks after I came home, my period started like clockwork. I told Hardy I had bad cramps and took a Tylenol. By morning, I could barely move. At work I squirmed through customers, massaging my pelvis under my jacket, shrinking into myself. My manager suggested I go to the ER. I went, handed over a cup for urine, and sat in the lobby amid strangers, squirming uncomfortably in pain.

They called me back eventually but didn't have a room open. They sat me in a chair by the nurses' station, the kind that fold out for old people, plush and wrong for someone who felt like they'd been hollowed from inside. Nurses, doctors, and EMTs pushed gurneys around me as I tried to minimize my pain and control my squirms.

After 20 minutes, I was given a room. A nurse came in and told me my lab results were normal, except one. "You're pregnant," she said statically. The words should have been everything I'd ever wanted, but I knew something was wrong as I waited for her to finish talking. "Ectopic," she suggested, the word soft, clinical, and full of menace. They scheduled bloodwork, ultrasounds, and appointments almost every morning for the following week.

"Rest. Don't lift. Try not to worry," were the words of comfort I received. The nurse handed me a note for two days off work and turned to leave. It was then that it hit me, and my voice broke as I asked, "Ectopic means it can't be carried, right?" as I tried to hold off the tears.

The nurse tried to reassure me, but the damage was done. I walked out to my car and sobbed quietly in the empty parking lot. I sat there in silence as the tears fell uncontrollably. I was broken, but I still had to muster up the courage to drive back home. That night my world felt still. Time crept as a million thoughts raced through my mind.

Morning came, and I headed out to my appointment, numb from the emotions of the night before. I sat impatiently waiting for the news no one wants to hear, but the new gyno smiled in a way that surprised me.

"No," she breathed, not the same no as before but a small, hopeful one. My numbers had risen. I'd rested. I seemed better. "Maybe, just maybe, this could be carried," she said with optimism.

I hesitated, second-guessing her words, not allowing myself to believe it. I had been let down too many times to let hope in.

Hopeful or not, the pain persisted. I kept working through it until I couldn't. Six days after that first ER visit, I had a follow-up. I wasn't greeted by the same doctor and confusion set in as another doctor told me, softly and then with a professional finish, "We are sorry, but you are having an ectopic pregnancy."

There it was. The words I feared were now a reality. The room thinned. My jaw quivered. She said the words in the way surgeons say things that will change you: urgent, nonnegotiable. "This pregnancy is unviable and life-threatening. We need to get you into surgery right away."

I called Hardy with my voice barely a whisper as I broke the news. He came to me, and together we sat in the parking lot, hands clenched like lifelines, staring at nothing. Our dream was slipping away, and neither of us could move. I needed just a few more minutes with my baby, just a few more breaths. I wasn't ready to say goodbye, not now, not ever.

I let out one last cry as I walked defeatedly into the hospital. It was one of the most traumatic experiences of my life. I was quickly taken back and stripped of everything, including my pride, as I removed all my jewelry and put on a paper gown and hair net. Several nurses surrounded me, each doing all they could to comfort me in those moments. After they finished prepping me, they left quietly as I sat there in silence staring at the wall across the room.

Hardy grabbed my hand and squeezed as the tears welled up in my eyes and fell silently down my face. Once my vision cleared, I could see everyone was staring at me.

One nurse grabbed a box of tissues and walked toward me, "I know this is hard," she whispered as she handed me the box. I began to cry even more as they wheeled me back and out of Hardy's sight.

The OR felt like a bright, alien sky full of masked faces and harsh lights. They told me they would intubate me. I was scared, and they promised that I wouldn't remember the procedure and that it would all be over soon. Those were promises that they couldn't keep. A few moments later, the drugs pulled me under.

When I awoke, it was in a sheer panic. As they struggled to frantically pull the tube from my throat my chest lunged forward as if my body was trying to scream. Nurses surrounded me, hushed and professional. I was being held and read to in medical terms while I clawed at air and light, desperate for answers as I drifted in and out of consciousness.

I woke in a recovery room with three small incisions and a feeling like I'd been shot. Pain lanced across my abdomen in bolts. They pushed pain meds, and for minutes I melted into something softer, but sleep brought convulsions and spasms I didn't know the name of. I winced and moaned in pain as I tried to grieve my loss.

They gave me a red folder with photos from the procedure as a keepsake. They were proof of prayers that were answered, but not fully realized. These weren't ultrasound pictures, there was no tiny head or hand to see, only sterile evidence of what had been inside me and the dreams I had lost that day. I keep that folder tucked away and glance at it on rare, heavy days. I can't look long as the wound of that loss cut deeper than the scalpel did.

Everything after was a slow burn. My recovery was not an easy one. My body felt like a balloon, bloated and swollen, and the slightest movements pulled and stretched my skin. My insides felt like they were on fire. My body wanted to give out, but I kept pushing through the nightmare my life had become. I sat alone and battled the dark thoughts that frequently entered my mind.

My first day back at work felt like a stranger's life. People thought I had quit. Nobody asked where I had been or if I was okay. The world just carried on, while mine shattered. My hands shook from pain and grief and the grit of trying to appear functional. At night, the what-ifs crawled up my spine: What would this child have looked like? Would I have been a good mother? Did I do something to deserve this? Sometimes the mind reaches for blame because if there is a reason, acceptance can happen, and the pain can ease. The reality is it doesn't. It never fades.

Now, months later, the incision aches like an old wound on windy days. There are moments when grief tightens my chest at random. The wound is more than flesh; it is a space in my life that holds both a person I loved and a future I wanted so badly.

But this is not all sorrow. I am grateful for the dream that kept me fighting, grateful for Hardy who held me through the nights of shaking and pain, grateful for the business that kept my mind engaged and the tiny victories that stitched me back stronger.

It is tempting to tell myself that this was all a bad dream, but the reality is my baby was real. This is their story. The brief time they were inside me mattered. Their story will forever be a part of mine. I hope that by sharing it others will be reminded that they are not alone.

To anyone who has felt the same sharp, private kind of loss: You are not broken. You are not abnormal. Your grief is not your fault. We are not alone in this. We may hurt, but we are *not* broken.

Carried for a Moment, Remembered for a Lifetime

From the time I was a little girl, motherhood was sewn into me like a secret thread. My dolls weren't just toys; they were my first children. I gave them names, whispered stories to them, lined them up on my bed like a tiny congregation of hope. I cradled them in the crook of my arm, their plastic heads warm from the sun shining through my bedroom window. At night, I'd tuck them in, my small hands mimicking the motions I imagined my mother making for me. Even then, before I fully knew what life was, I knew this: I wanted to be a mom.

By the time I fell in love during my senior year, that dream had grown roots. We'd sit on the rooftop, staring at the stars, talking about our future. Marriage. Our first house. Babies. I wanted them young. I wanted my home full of the sounds of squealing laughter and pattering feet before I even fully understood adulthood. What I didn't know then was how cruel hope can become when it stretches over years without fulfillment.

Seven years.

Seven years of peeing on sticks and lining them up on the bathroom counter like tiny gravestones.

Seven years of whispering prayers into the quiet dark of our bedroom.

Seven years of waiting for one day late to turn into two, into a lifetime.

Seven years of negatives carving little holes in my heart, month after month after month.

By the time February 2022 arrived, I'd stopped letting myself dream. I was in Florida, caring for my grandmother who had just been diagnosed with stage 4 lung cancer. The house smelled like ocean salt and antiseptic, a mix of hope and endings. My period was one day late. Just one.

Normally, I would have ignored it. But something in me, a flicker of old instinct, pushed me.

I drove to the tiny Dollar General on the island, my palms sweating as I reached for a box of Clear Blue tests. The cardboard felt heavy, like it held my whole future inside. In my grandma's bathroom with the tile cool beneath my bare feet, I waited. And then, as if by magic, it appeared, a faint plus sign. My breath caught. My heart pounded so loud I could hear it echoing in my ears. After seven long years, there it was. The yes I'd been waiting for.

I snapped a picture and sent it to my husband with trembling hands. His reply was cautious, unsure, as he was colorblind and didn't see what I saw.

My uncle dismissed it completely, "You're just seeing what you want to see." His words stung like salt in an open wound.

But my aunt, looking at the test in my hand, placed her palm on my arm and whispered, "That's a positive, Nay."

In that moment, I felt the universe burst open. Someone else *saw it too*. I wasn't crazy. I wasn't imagining. I was pregnant.

Over the next few days, I took test after test, lining them up like little soldiers of hope. I whispered to myself at night, "It'll get darker. It'll get darker." For the first time in years, I went to bed smiling.

Then on February 22, I woke to blood. Dark, heavy, metallic. My stomach dropped. My heart knew before my head did. I called my husband, my voice trembling, panic rising in my throat. He told me to go to the ER.

I didn't even have pads, so I stuffed toilet paper into my underwear. My hands shook so hard I could barely drive. The smell of iron filled the car, mixing with my tears. My body felt like it was betraying me in the cruelest way.

At the ER, the nurse confirmed it: I was pregnant, but I was miscarrying. Her words echoed in my ears, muffled, like I was underwater. I called my husband, and we both cried, clinging to the bittersweet fact that I had finally gotten pregnant, and the crushing truth that I wouldn't get to keep the baby we'd already begun to love.

When I returned for follow-up labs, a different nurse sat me in a hallway chair. There was no privacy, just cold fluorescent lights buzzing overhead. His voice was kind but detached as he confirmed my loss. "How much stress have you been under lately?" he asked. I wanted to scream. As if my grief had caused this. As if it were my fault.

But the deepest cut came when I told my grandmother. I sat in the rocking chair beside her bed, the wood creaking softly under my weight, tears streaming silently down my face. She turned to me, eyes wet, her voice quiet. "Can I tell you something?"

"Sure," I whispered, bracing myself.

"I didn't want you to be pregnant so you didn't have to leave me."

My heart splintered. Her words carved through me like glass. The woman I loved most, my anchor, my safe place, had tied my loss to her need. I wanted to scream, to run, to crumble. Instead, I just nodded, numbed by pain. In that moment, I decided: If I couldn't have my baby, she couldn't have me. I had to leave.

Back in Ohio, silence became my constant companion. My husband confessed his guilt one night, blurting out words I never expected: "Maybe if I hadn't been watching so much porn we would've gotten pregnant sooner."

I blinked at him, stunned. My mind replayed every night I cried to him about hating my body, every appointment, every pill, every moment I blamed myself. And now this. My world cracked open again.

Both halves of my heart, my grandma and my husband, had shattered. Numbness filled my days.

My baby was gone.

My family was fractured.

My marriage was cracking.

Grief became a storm with no end. Nights stretched long and endless. I wept into pillows, whispering, "My baby, my baby, I want my baby." Due dates came and went like knives twisting in an open wound. October 26, 2022, a day that should have been filled with balloons, smiles, and tiny cries was just silence. Just me, alone with the painful memories.

That's why I tell my story now. Because miscarriage is a lonely, suffocating grief. People don't talk about it. They look away. They move on while you sit with an ache that never leaves. I share because I know what it feels like to think no one cares. To feel like you failed. To stare at a test and a calendar with a broken heart, wondering if you'll ever feel whole again.

I may never have children. My marriage is over. My family is fractured in ways that may never mend. But I hold on to one hope that keeps me breathing and pushing forward: One day, in Heaven, I'll hear a small voice call out to me, "Mom, I'm here. I've been waiting for you." In that instant, my heart will be whole again.

If you are reading this, carrying the same hollow ache in your chest, please know this: Your grief is real. Your love is real. Your child, no matter how briefly carried, is real. There is no timeline for this kind of loss, no moving on, only moving forward with the love that will forever live inside you.

Some days, the weight will feel unbearable. Other days, it will feel lighter, but through it all, your baby's memory will remain. Even in your silence, even in your tears, even in your aching prayers whispered into the dark, you are still a mother.

I may have only carried you for a moment, but I'll remember you for a lifetime.

Nevaeh's Orchard

It was right after my birthday when the two little lines appeared. I had just returned from Egypt with the red desert sand still clinging to my suitcase and the taste of adventure still on my tongue.

For eight years, we had waited for this moment, another baby, another chance to grow our family. When I saw the test, my breath caught in my chest, partly with wonder, partly with fear. My hands shook as I pressed them against my belly, whispering, "Is this really happening?"

But even as joy surged, doubt crept in. We were about to move across states, leaving behind every ounce of support we had known. Could I really do this while living nomadically, far from home, far from help? My heart was a pendulum swinging wildly between excitement and anxiety. Still, I chose hope. I pivoted, just like I always did, and began to imagine what life would look like with another little heartbeat in our family.

Yet something felt different. With my other two pregnancies, I dreamt vivid dreams. I could see my babies' faces before they arrived, feel their genders whispered in my spirit. This time, though, I felt a strange distance, like I was standing outside a window, watching my own story unfold from behind the glass. Looking back now, I wonder if my body already knew what my heart refused to believe, if it was quietly building walls to protect me from what was coming.

When we shared the news, the people around us erupted with joy. Our families had been begging us for years to have another baby. We made a silly, sweet video, the "choose your player" trend, announcing that we were adding one more teammate. Their happiness was contagious, and for a while, it drowned out my doubts.

Then came the moment that made my stomach twist. At my last doctor's appointment in New Hampshire, just before our big move, the Doppler couldn't find a heartbeat. The doctor smiled softly and said it was probably just too early, that I shouldn't worry. I clung to that reassurance like a lifeline, even though something deep inside of me whispered otherwise. I pushed the thought away. We were moving. We had no time to stop, no time to break.

A few weeks later, in South Carolina, the bleeding started. It was light at first, easy to explain away. But then it grew heavier, darker, more insistent. My body was speaking the truth I didn't want to hear. At the ER, the word *miscarriage* slipped from the doctor's lips, heavy and final. They sent me home with instructions, but the bleeding didn't stop. It only grew worse.

That night, at 1:00 a.m., I was rushed back. The world blurred into fluorescent lights and hurried footsteps. The metallic scent of blood filling the air. As they wheeled me toward the ultrasound, I turned to the tech, my voice trembling. "I'm going to die. Please call for help."

Then everything broke open. My body convulsed, and suddenly I was upside down in a wheelchair with vomit covering me and the world spinning away. A nurse's face came into focus, eyes wide and urgent, "We lost you for a moment." In that sliver of nothingness, I heard a voice, steady and undeniable, "It is not your time. You still have so much work to do."

When I woke again, the doctor confirmed what I already knew. The baby was gone. My Nevaeh. Heaven, spelled backward.

The days that followed were a blur. I bled for weeks as my body emptied itself of dreams it was never allowed to hold. I lay in bed, weak and helpless, clutching the tiny onesies I had bought, pressing the soft fabric to my chest as if it could fill the hollow inside me. All I had left of her was a single ultrasound picture, a grainy outline of what could have been.

Anger consumed me. Grief settled heavy in my bones, a constant ache that no one else could see. Yet, in the midst of it all, people showed up. Our new friends in South Carolina became family, sitting with us in the silence, listening without judgment. My clients wrapped me in grace, allowing me space to crumble and slowly come together again.

Through it all, my two older children were my anchor. They were in the hospital during much of it, their small faces grounding me in the land of the living. Their father stood beside me, steady, loving, reminding me that I was not alone.

Nevaeh's short life changed everything. She made me look at relationships differently, trimming away those that drained me and clinging tighter to the ones who showed up in my darkest hour. She brought me closer to God, to a faith that whispered of purpose, even in loss.

Out of my grief, I built something in her honor: Nevaeh's Orchard, a nonprofit that carries her memory forward. It is my way of ensuring her story, though brief, bears fruit, and is never forgotten.

We talk about her every day. When butterflies appear, I know it is her, reminding me she is never far. She has a younger sister now, and together we keep her legacy alive, proof that love never dies, even when dreams are interrupted.

If I could tell another mother going through this what I have learned, I would tell her this: Do not hold your story in silence. Speak your baby's name. Share your grief. You are not alone. Your child matters. Your love for them still matters.

Nevaeh may not be here in my arms, but she is everywhere else, in the flutter of wings, in the orchard that grows in her honor, in the love that deepened because she existed. And because of her, I will never stop telling our story.

Always Remembered

The evening of October 21, 2025, was quiet, warm, and full of anticipation. I was four days past my due date with our second son, Jason. The weight of him rested heavy and low, my belly full with promise.

That night, like so many nights before, I reached for the Doppler with excitement. Hearing his strong heartbeat had always been my favorite reassurance, that steady rhythm filling me with peace. But when I placed the doppler against my skin, the room fell into silence with no thump-thump, no echo of life that had always been so easy to find.

We tried again, and again. Nothing. My husband and I brushed it off, telling ourselves it was probably just the late stage of pregnancy, too crowded for the Doppler to catch him. Still, unease lingered. Forty-five minutes later, when I stood to use the bathroom, I noticed a small streak of blood. *It's time, the beginning stages of labor,* I told myself.

My chest tightened. I called for my husband, my voice shaking as he dialed the nurse on call. We packed our hospital bags and Jason's diaper bag with his little outfits carefully folded inside, ready to wrap around a body we longed to hold. We hugged our three-year-old son and our family, whispering promises that when we came back through that door, we would be a family of four.

The drive to the hospital was surreal. My husband and I held hands and spoke softly about how the night had finally come, how soon Jason would be in our arms. The air in the car was heavy with hope, thick with dreams, as we pictured our future with him.

At the hospital, I checked in, pacing nervously until they called my name. I kissed my husband and told him I'd see him soon. Inside the room, I slipped into the gown, the cool air brushing my bare skin. The nurse spread warm gel across my belly and pressed the Doppler down. Silence. I told her to try the right side, where Jason had nestled most of the pregnancy. Again, silence. My heart sank, my face drained of color. My worse fears were confirmed.

The nurse went to get the doctor and promised to send my husband back. When he walked into the room, his smile lit the space, pure joy radiating from his face. He didn't yet know. My voice broke as I told him something was wrong. He squeezed my hand tightly, whispering, "Don't panic. It's going to be okay." But his voice wavered, thin and uncertain.

The doctor entered, performed the ultrasound, and after a long silence, spoke the words that will forever echo in my bones, "I'm so sorry. There's no heartbeat."

The world shattered. My husband and I clung to each other, sobbing, pieces of our hearts falling into the sterile floor. Between sobs, I apologized to him, as if somehow my body had failed us both, as if this cruel twist of fate was mine to carry alone. The doctor, face full of sorrow, gently explained our next steps, then left us to grieve.

I called my sister. She answered with excitement, ready for good news. Instead, I cried out the words no one should ever have to say, "Your nephew has no heartbeat." My sobs filled the silence that followed. I asked her to tell our parents, our siblings. I couldn't say it again.

We were moved upstairs, where Pitocin dripped into my veins, coaxing my body into labor. The staff asked us questions I never imagined I'd have to answer: Did we want to hold him right away? Should they place him on my chest or swaddle him first? Did my husband want to cut the cord? Pictures, during birth or after? Burial or cremation? Autopsy or not? Bloodwork from me, from Jason? Each decision tore another hole in my already broken heart. Never, not once in all my dreams of motherhood, had I thought I'd sit with my husband discussing how we'd lay our newborn son to rest before he was even born.

The hours crawled by in aching silence with no comforting whoosh of Jason's heartbeat on the monitor, just emptiness. My husband and I held hands, resting against each other, our grief suspended in the stillness.

At 6:42 a.m. on October 22nd, after eight short minutes of pushing, Jason entered the world. He weighed 8 pounds, 2 ounces. He was beautiful. He was peaceful. He was everything we had dreamed he would be, except for the life in his chest.

We held him. Kissed him. Took pictures. Whispered apologies into his soft skin. Made promises that he would never be forgotten, that his name would always be spoken, that he was, and always will be, so loved.

Family came, tears mixing with tenderness as they held him, their grandson, their nephew, saying goodbye before hello. Our three-year-old son met his little brother, a bittersweet moment tangled with love and loss. So many emotions filled that room.

Then came the hardest goodbye. Watching nurses roll Jason's small body toward the elevator, down to the morgue instead of out the doors with us, broke me in ways words cannot capture.

The days that followed blurred together. My body ached from labor, my heart from loss. We arranged his cremation, picked him up, and gave him the only celebration of life we'd ever be able to offer. We baptized him, dedicated him to the Lord, spoke a eulogy for the boy we would never raise.

In the months since, my husband and I have clung to one another, choosing to heal together. Our families, friends, and community surrounded us with love and grace. For Jason's first birthday, we planned acts of remembrance: a donation basket for the hospital, a cake with family, balloons released to the sky, whispers of love from the three of us who remain earthside.

There is not a day we don't think of Jason. His absence is as present as our love for him, and yet we believe he is with us. He shows up in dreams, in cardinals, in quiet moments when the veil feels thin.

Recently, we discovered I am pregnant again, something we never expected naturally after years of IVF. We know this is a gift, one touched by both God and Jason's hands.

Jason's story is one of heartbreak, but also one of love unmeasured. Although his life was brief, it was infinite in meaning. He will forever be our son, our angel, our reminder that the smallest moments can leave an internal impact. He will be with us forever, always loved, always remembered, always a part of our family.

The Little Girl with the Red Hair

We had waited a long time to start a family. We'd done all the things a couple does before taking that next step. We'd built a house; we'd built a life.

I still remember our trip to Disney World. On the last day, with the sun dipping low behind Cinderella Castle and the sound of music and happy families in the hot evening air, I threw away my birth control pills. I struck a pose and smiled for my husband's camera.

Within a few months, I was pregnant. It didn't occur to me for a second to worry. I had never known anyone who had a miscarriage. I certainly never imagined it would happen to me.

Full of naïve optimism, we had a party for our family. I carefully selected and wrapped gifts to surprise them with our good news. I learned a hard lesson that day: Never tell anyone good news if you don't want to have to tell them bad news.

After the miscarriage, my husband repeated over and over and over robotically, "I'm okay. You're okay. We're going to be okay."

Looking back, I think he was trying to convince himself. It didn't work.

Within days, he unraveled, and our marriage dissolved. I couldn't even think about the miscarriage because I was trying so hard to save our marriage. That also didn't work.

Just two years later, I met my second husband. When I became pregnant, I didn't tell anyone. *Certainly lightning wouldn't strike twice,* I thought.

But once again, the spark that had ignited inside me went out too soon. Another miscarriage. Another husband distanced, barely spoke of the loss and offered little hope for the future. He might not have *physically* left that day, but he might as well have.

I got pregnant for the third time easily, and that time it was different. My son was born, and 21 months later, his brother arrived. "The two children I always wanted," I've said many times. But as I type that, a tiny part of me wonders, *And the other two?*

Years later, something strange happened.

I had a close friend who's psychic. She had told me things over the years that proved true, things no one else could have known.

One afternoon, as we talked on the phone, she interrupted me mid-sentence.

"Do you sometimes feel something tugging at your wrist?" she asked.

That surprised me. "Actually, yes," I said. My mother had given me a Pandora bracelet, the kind with a heavy snake chain, and she had gifted me many charms over the years. I didn't wear it often, especially when I was working because the weight of it was distracting. It often felt like it was being pulled down.

My friend's voice grew softer. "I keep seeing a little girl there, tugging at something. Now she's pointing at your stomach. She's insistent, like she's trying to tell me something. But I don't understand it."

My psychic friend kept telling me she was trying to push the little girl out of her mind to answer the questions I kept peppering her with, questions about the future of my challenging marriage and my stressful job. I could tell she was really distracted though.

Then it hit me.

"Astrid, I don't think I ever told you, but I've had two miscarriages. Could the little girl be one of those babies, trying to tell you she used to be *in* my stomach? Do you ever see spirits of babies who were miscarried?"

"Yes," Astrid said, hesitating as if she was still trying to make sense of it herself. "She's about eight years old. She has long, straight red hair—not the *pretty* red, but a really *orangey* red. She's twirling around and around and around—and smiling."

That got me. The red hair, the hair that ran in our family that my mother always joked she thought one of my kids would have.

"Do you think that could be her? One of the babies I lost?"

Astrid's tone softened. "Yes."

A few years passed, busy and filled with the laughter of my two sons, now eight and six, full of energy and life.

Out of the blue, despite always being healthy, my Pap tests began coming back abnormal. Puzzled but playing it safe, my doctor recommended having a hysterectomy.

"It's what I would do," she said, knowing we were both around the same age and our families were complete. I agreed, happy to have the issue resolved and get on with my life.

The hysterectomy and recovery went well. I waited impatiently in the surgeon's office for my one-month checkup, once again naïvely expecting all would be fine. In fact, I was so certain of it, we had planned to leave right from the doctor's office to a few days at the beach.

I was completely unprepared when my doctor came into the room and said, "To my surprise, we found a cancer." He patiently answered the few questions that popped into my mind, then said the words I'll always remember. "This is going to change your life in many ways. And they won't all be bad."

Although the train of my life had just completely jumped the tracks, I decided we might as well go to the beach as planned. Why ruin my husband and my sons' vacation? So we went.

Almost 20 years later, when I see photos from that trip come up on my TV or phone, I'm relieved to see my sons looking happy and carefree. They seemed completely unaware how much life was about to change.

We stayed at a tiny inn—not much bigger than a house with only a handful of guest rooms. I remember our room was on the second floor, right at the top of the stairs. On the last day of our trip, my sons were napping, and their dad offered to stay in the room with them, while I shuttled a few things down to our SUV.

On my last trip back upstairs, as I reached the landing outside our room, I was surprised to see a little girl standing there. She looked to be about eight years old, with long, red hair and a hint of freckles dusting her nose.

I was a little dismayed to see bright ovals of sunburn under the little girl's eyes, like the grease football players apply to block the sun's glare or the paint a warrior might apply before battle. *What's wrong with this little girl's mother, not putting on her sunscreen properly?* I thought.

As I took the few steps from the stairs to the door of our room, the little girl didn't move. I smiled and said gently, "This is our room, dear."

She stared up at me, wide-eyed.

"I need to get past you, please," I said, edging closer to the door and reaching for the knob with my right hand.

The little girl paid no attention, and in fact, she seemed determined to push *past* me to get into our room. Feeling a little frayed and eager to get in to the room to see what my sons were up to, I quickly opened the door, brushed past the little girl, and closed the door behind me.

I don't remember what happened next, but likely I was bombarded with my sons' happy energy and responsibilities to get them and the car packed so we could head back to our home, to the long list of treatments and doctor's visits that had been hinted at by the surgeon just a few days before.

A short while later, perhaps while I was driving and my husband and sons were fast asleep, it occurred to me: *Could that have been her?*

After we had all been settled back home a few days later, I drove to an empty parking lot in a quiet park at dusk. I called Astrid and described what had happened. "Do you think it was her?"

"Did she speak?" Astrid asked.

"No. Why?" I asked.

"Because sometimes it takes spirits so much energy to become visible, they can't speak too."

The little girl hadn't spoken. Looking back, I'm astonished at how closely she resembled my sons. I believe the sunburns under her eyes were actually warpaint—her only way to express to me:

"You've got this, Mom. I'm fighting right beside you."

A Closing Word

Every story shared here is a testimony of hope, heartbreak, resilience, and love. Whether it was the first faint line on a pregnancy test that felt like a miracle or the silence of a doctor's office where a heartbeat should have been, each moment is carved deep into memory. These stories, though different in details, echo one another. They remind us that loss is not a solitary path, even though it feels like it in the moment.

I know what it feels like to sit in the car after the news, clutching your stomach as if you can somehow hold on just a little longer. I know what it feels like to stare at tiny onesies in your drawer, wondering if they will ever be worn. I know the silence of a house that feels emptier than it should, the ache in your chest when the calendar reminds you of due dates that will never come.

But I also know the strength that rises quietly in the middle of it all. The way grief can forge resilience. The way love for our babies, whether carried for weeks, months, or only in our dreams, never disappears. Our children live in the ways we remember them, in the whispers of their names, in the butterflies that pass us on warm days, in the work we do to honor them.

If you are reading this and have walked this road, I want you to know you are not alone. Your grief is valid. Your love is real. Your story matters. Sometimes the most powerful healing comes not from silence, but from sharing. Speaking the names of our babies, telling the truth of our pain, and finding community in those who understand.

That's why I created my podcast, Echoes of Love. It's a place where these stories can be spoken, honored, and held with tenderness. Because every echo of love matters, and together, our voices remind us that hope still exists, even in heartbreak.

If you feel called to share your story, I would be honored to hold space for you. You can reach out to me directly at *jayme.echoesoflove@gmail.com* to be a guest on the podcast.

Your story is sacred. Your baby is remembered. And you, dear friend, are deeply loved.

Remembering October

October is Pregnancy and Infant Loss Awareness Month, first declared by President Ronald Reagan in 1988. This month will always hold deep meaning for me. It is a time to pause and remember our babies gone too soon, to honor their short but powerful lives, and to stand hand in hand with families who carry this same grief.

If you have lost your baby, please know this: Your story matters, your love matters, and your baby's life matters. Sharing their name, their memory, and your journey helps break the silence and lets others know they are not alone. For those who have walked alongside a loved one in their loss, your compassion has been a gift more valuable than you may ever know.

This October, I invite you to honor your baby in a way that feels meaningful to you, such as by lighting a candle on October 15 for the Wave of Light, wearing pink and blue, creating something beautiful in their memory, performing a random act of kindness, or simply whispering their name into the quiet. Each gesture, no matter how small, carries great weight. It keeps their legacy alive, opens hearts to compassion, and helps build a world where grieving families feel seen and supported.

This book is my way of honoring our losses. I hope that these stories have reminded you that love is greater than loss, that although our babies are not in our arms, they will always be in our hearts. Together, our voices and our memories ensure their lives will never be forgotten.

These are our Echoes of Love, whispers of our babies carried forward in the stories we tell, the acts of kindness we do, and the lives we continue to live in their honor.

From my heart to yours, may you feel your baby's love echoing around you, today and always. Never stop sharing their echoes with the world.

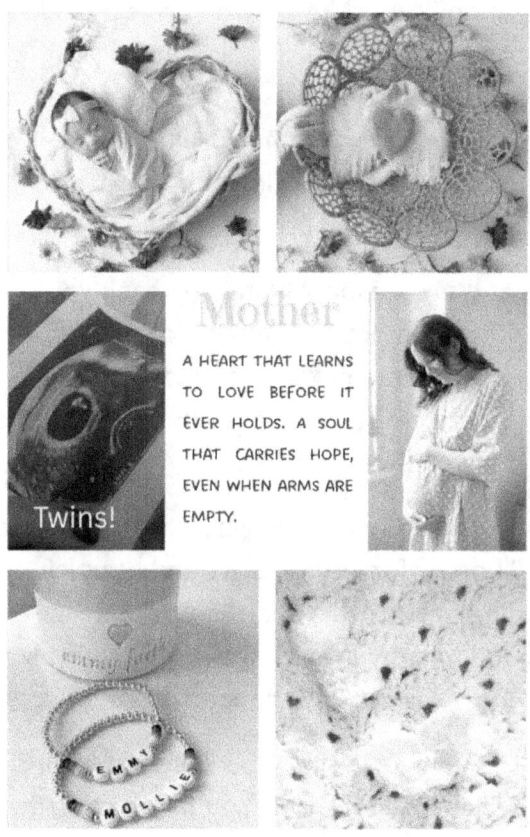

Acknowledgments

To all the women who so bravely shared their stories—thank you. Without your courage, this book would not exist. Each of you opened your heart, exposed your pain, and in doing so, created something that will touch countless lives. I hope that telling your story brought healing and that you carry peace in knowing your loved ones are remembered and honored on these pages.

To my husband and two children who are earthside—you are my heart and my purpose. Thank you for your love, patience, and understanding as I've grieved, written, and healed. Your support has given me strength to keep going and to be a light for others walking a similar path. I love you more than words can express.

To The Blox and my Season 23 family—thank you for inspiring me to want more for myself. For reading my rough drafts, crying with me, and reminding me that vulnerability is strength. You believed in me before I did, and for that, I am endlessly grateful.

A special thank you to Jennifer Bright, a fellow Bloxer and dear friend. I'll never forget our tears and heartfelt conversation in the airport. Your encouragement, compassion, and publishing guidance helped turn my vision into reality. Great things truly happen when Bloxers unite.

To God—thank You for placing this calling in my heart. I heard You loud and clear. Thank You for trusting me to bring light to what is often left in silence. Every word written here is for You, through You, and because of You.

Last but not least, I want to extend my deepest gratitude to all the companies and organizations listed below for standing beside families who have known the pain of pregnancy and infant loss. Your compassion, awareness, and dedication help bring comfort to those walking through unimaginable grief. Thank you for using your voices, your platforms, and your hearts to remind the world that these little lives mattered—and still do. Together, we are breaking the silence.

Project
Robby

Helping families with Angel Babies

Making
a
Miracle

NEVAEH'S ORCHARD

Echoes
of Love
PODCAST

Share
Pregnancy & Infant Loss Support

www.ingramcontent.com/pod-product-compliance
Lightning Source LLC
Chambersburg PA
CBHW071523120626
46550CB00006B/2334